SCHOOL & FAMILY PARTNERSHIPS

Case Studies for Regular and Special Educators

SCHOOL & FAMILY PARTNERSHIPS

Case Studies for Regular and Special Educators

Judith Brachman Buzzell
Southern Connecticut State University

Delmar Publishers

I(T)P™ An International Thomson Publishing Company

Albany • Bonn • Boston • Cincinnati • Detroit • London • Madrid
Melbourne • Mexico City • New York • Pacific Grove • Paris
San Francisco • Singapore • Tokyo • Toronto • Washington

Cover Design: The Drawing Board

Delmar Staff
Publisher: Diane McOscar
Administrative Editor: Jay Whitney
Associate Editor: Erin J. O'Connor Traylor

Production Coordinator: James Zayicek
Art & Design Coordinator: Carol Keohane
Project Editor: Timothy Coleman

Copyright © 1996
By Delmar Publishers
a division of International Thomson Publishing Inc.

The ITP logo is a trademark under license

Printed in the United States of America

For more information, contact:

Delmar Publishers
3 Columbia Circle, Box 15015
Albany, New York 12212-5015

International Thomson Publishing Europe
Berkshire House 168-173
High Holborn
London, WC1V7AA
England

Thomas Nelson Australia
102 Dodds Street
South Melbourne, 3205
Victoria, Australia

Nelson Canada
1120 Birchmount Road
Scarborough, Ontario
Canada M1K 5G4

International Thomson Editores
Campos Eliseos 385, Piso 7
Col Polanco
11560 Mexico D F Mexico

International Thomson Publishing Gmbh
Königswinterer Strasse 418
53227 Bonn
Germany

International Thomson Publishing Asia
221 Henderson Road #05-10
Henderson Building
Singapore 0315

International Thomson Publishing - Japan
Hirakawacho Kyowa Building, 3F
2-2-1 Hirakawacho
Chiyoda-ku, 102 Tokyo
Japan

1 2 3 4 5 6 7 8 9 10 XXX 01 00 99 98 97 96 95

Library of Congress Cataloging-in-Publication Data

Buzzell, Judith B.
    School & family partnerships : case studies for regular and
special educators / Judith Brachman Buzzell.
        p.   cm.
    Includes bibliographical references and index.
    ISBN 0-8273-7163-2
    1. Home and school--United States--Case studies.   2. Parent
-teacher relationships--United States--Case studies.   3. Special
education--Parent participation--United States--Case studies.
I. Title.
LC225.3.B777   1996
370.19'312--dc20   95-26621
                                                            CIP

This book is dedicated
to my son, Joshua,
who has taught me
many lessons.

Contents

Preface

Over the past 30 years, a growing body of research has testified to the benefits of school and family partnerships. When parents become involved with their children's education, working in concert with teachers and administrators, everyone gains—especially the children. Inviting parents to get involved is not without its pitfalls (as this book will show), but on balance their participation is a positive and even necessary component of effective early childhood and elementary education. Ideally, parents get to know teachers as people and develop respect for the teaching role. They often build their parenting skills and self-confidence. Teachers feel appreciated by such parents, and they may build relationships that lead to tangible help in their classrooms. Schools benefit from the resources, services and community support that parents can provide. And, most important, children's academic performance and social behavior improve.

I am a teacher of aspiring teachers and of experienced teachers who are for the most part working toward graduate degrees in education. For the past several years I have taught a graduate course on parent involvement in education. When I first began teaching the course, I would enthusiastically recount for my students the research supporting school and family partnerships. I described the many effective family involvement programs in place around the country, and shared a profusion of proven strategies to involve parents in schools. Both the novice and experienced teachers in the class would dutifully nod their heads, apparently agreeing.

But when my students began to talk about their own teaching experiences, they were far less sanguine about the feasibility of parent-teacher partnerships. Some were baffled by parent behaviors. How could parents take their kids out of school for a week to go on a family vacation? Others were angered to witness just how lightly certain parents seemed to take their responsibilities. How could they let their children stay up late watching violent television shows? How could parents arrive at school drunk to pick up their children?

When I suggested inviting parents into the classroom as volunteers to read stories to children or help with art projects, several students rolled their eyes. Why invite the scrutiny of outsiders?

Rather than seeing parents as partners in the task of raising healthy children, many teachers viewed them as outright adversaries. Surprisingly, teachers who were parents themselves sometimes expressed this "us against them" stance. Even these teacher-parents—who I would have expected to be enthusiastic about family involvement in schools—were instead skeptical.

Admittedly, in the best of circumstances, fostering effective family involvement takes a concerted effort. There are obstacles to overcome for both parents and teachers. Parents may not have enough free time, particularly when both are employed. Single parents are usually even more stretched for time.

Parents may not consider themselves on an equal footing with teachers. They may feel intimidated about asking for advice on how to encourage their children's learning. If they had unhappy school experiences as children themselves, they may regard teachers with suspicion or even fear.

There are obstacles for teachers as well. They too may lack time to nurture relationships with families because they are busy juggling home and other teaching responsibilities. They may not have been trained to work effectively with families. In facing difficult encounters with parents, they may lack adequate support from personnel in their school.

Moreover, there may be cultural barriers between the two groups. American families are diverse, and teachers and parents may speak different languages, practice different customs, and hold different values. Both teachers and parents may have deeply embedded—and sometimes unconscious— racial, religious, or class biases. These biases can make effective communication and cooperation difficult, if not impossible.

As I listened to my students' comments, I realized that it wasn't enough to simply tell them that parent-teacher partnerships were a great idea. Even the reports of thirty years of research were unlikely to change their attitudes. I needed to show them—and they needed to see—something more concrete and engaging: real people grappling with specific problems.

About this time, I had begun to write case studies, based on interviews with and observations of teachers, and to use them in my courses. These culminated in the textbook I wrote with Robert Piazza, *Case Studies for Teaching Special Needs and At-Risk Students* (1994). I had observed, as others have, that the case method seemed particularly effective in preparing teachers emotionally for the demanding situations they might encounter. I suspected that this approach would be useful in tempering the kinds of negative judgments my students might make about family involvement in schools.

Case studies have the virtue of simulating involvement while offering distance. One encounters these people and their problems vicariously. With nothing personal at stake in the encounter, the student is freed to think creatively. I believe that by working through the cases in this book, teachers can gain both the empathy and the problem-solving skills they need to work effectively with parents.

Indeed, in trying out the cases in my classes, I found that students began genuinely to feel parents' feelings and understand their behaviors. Even when discussing cases told from the point of view of a teacher who felt, for example, threatened by or angry at parents, students were able to sympathize with the parents. My students broadened their emotional horizons. They became capable of developing more caring, creative, and sophisticated solutions to the problems in the cases. Best of all, the stories they shared from their own experiences began to reflect this increased sensitivity. While they might not have agreed with a parent's perspective or behavior, they no longer offhandedly condemned the parents.

ORIENTATION TO THIS BOOK

Since promoting school and family partnerships is an important goal of both regular and special educators, this book is designed for both. The organization of cases makes it easy to use. Regular educators are the main characters in the cases in the first half of the book; the second half focuses on special issues or has special educators as the main characters. Many cases describe regular and special educators working together. All the cases focus on early childhood and elementary education.

I hope the book will be a helpful supplement in undergraduate and graduate courses on family involvement in schools in both regular and special education programs, as well as general courses in early childhood or elementary education. It should also prove useful for in-service workshops. Having used the cases with both preservice and veteran teachers, I have found that they can be effective teaching tools for students at different levels of experience.

I have based these cases on stories that teachers, parents, and administrators throughout Connecticut have shared with me. Some are composites. To maintain confidentiality, the names and locales have been changed. I have also modified other particulars.

The cases portray schools and families interacting in a variety of situations. They show parents and teachers communicating with each other, including conferencing. Educators collaborate with families of children at risk and children with special needs. They interact with families from culturally diverse groups. The cases depict parents, as aides or volunteers, working alongside teachers in classrooms. They describe parents taking an active role in making school policies, by serving on advisory committees.

The book is organized with the following features. The matrix on pages 000–00 assists the reader to quickly identify the important roles, topics, and issues in each case. The table of contents helps to identify these as well. The introductory chapter explains the debates surrounding the importance of family involvement in schools. It also describes the value of the case method in teacher education, and it walks students through steps to help analyze a case and prepare for a discussion.

Following each case, there are questions for discussion and follow-up activities. These help students to sharpen their analysis and to broaden their understanding. Finally, the list of selected readings at the end of the book provides background reading. The selections are organized along the main topics addressed in the cases.

The success of the case method as a teaching strategy relies on more than the quality of the cases. Just as important is a teacher's comfort with and skill at teaching in this nontraditional style. For this reason, I have prepared a separate *Instructor's Manual* to accompany this book. In it, I offer suggestions for teaching each case, providing a summary of each story, an analysis of major issues, and some possible lines of discussion. The *Instructor's Manual* is the result of field-testing the cases in teacher education classrooms.

ACKNOWLEDGMENTS

I am indebted to many colleagues, friends, and family members who have encouraged and supported this effort.

For initially kindling my interest in the case method and providing ongoing guidance, I thank my colleagues, Traci Bliss at the University of Kentucky and Judith Kleinfeld at the University of Alaska, Fairbanks.

Many administrators and faculty at Southern Connecticut State University have supported my efforts. I want to express appreciation particularly to Anthony Pinciaro, Vice President for Academic Affairs; Bernice Willis, former Dean of the School of Education; and Peter Barile, Chairperson of the Education Department, for providing research release time that was so crucial to the completion of this project. Robert Piazza and Elizabeth Johnston, colleagues in the Special Education Department, and Denise Rini of the Communication Disorders Department steadfastly encouraged and advised me. I am also grateful to Connecticut State University for providing grant monies for this project.

I would like to thank my reviewers for their insightful critiques, which led to a greatly improved text:

Lisa A. Bloom, Ph.D.
Western Carolina University
Cullowhee, NC

Joan M. Goodship, Ph.D.
University of Richmond
Richmond, VA

John H. Hoover, Ph.D.
University of North Dakota
Grand Forks, ND

Pat Hulsebosch, Ph.D.
National-Louis University
Chicago, IL

Lynne Steyer Noble, Ed.D.
University of South Carolina-Columbia
Columbia, SC

Karen F. Robertson, Ph.D.
University of South Carolina-
 Spartenburg
Spartanburg, SC

Elaine Traynelis-Yurek, Ed.D.
University of Richmond
Richmond, VA

Special thanks to Rosemary Yanosik for her careful typing of the manuscript. I am, of course, indebted to my editor at Delmar, Erin O'Connor Traylor, for her conscientious facilitation of this project.

My husband, Lloyd J. Buzzell, has shown unstinting support for my writing. He carefully reviewed each case and made discerning and clear-sighted recommendations. His previous experience as a student of the case method in business school was invaluable. I thank my friends, Robert Cole and Catherine Corman for editing sections of the book, thus bringing their keen intellects to bear on this project.

Most of all, I am indebted to the teachers, parents, and administrators who so generously shared their stories with me. Although, for reasons of confidentiality, I do not include their names, I want to thank them because they have contributed most profoundly to this book. Their willingness to share their insights, feelings, and knowledge on behalf of teacher education made this book possible.

ABOUT THE AUTHOR

Judith Brachman Buzzell, an Associate Professor in the Education Department of Southern Connecticut State University, has worked with children of all ages and their parents. She started her career teaching English at a New York City public high school. Subsequently, she helped to develop a Piagetian-based elementary school curriculum at Yale University and was a teacher and Assistant Director at the Gesell Institute Nursery School. At Southern Connecticut State University's laboratory school, she supervised student teachers and worked with children and families. Presently, she uses the case method in her teaching of early childhood education and secondary school methods courses, including a graduate course on family involvement in schools. She has written numerous articles and is the coauthor of *Case Studies for Teaching Special Needs and At-Risk Students* (Delmar, 1994).

Matrix of Cases

Case Title	A Conflict of Interest	The Butterfly	He'll Beat Me!	A Family Matter	Grounds for Divorce	The Bully	New Kid on the Block	Whose Problem Is It?	What More Can I Do?	How Much Parent Involvement Is Too Much?	Multicultural Misunderstanding
Case number	1	2	3	4	5	6	7	8	9	10	11
Regular educator	✓	✓	✓	✓	✓	✓	✓	✓	✓	✓	✓
Special educator											
Administrator				✓						✓	✓
Urban	✓	✓		✓	✓			✓	✓		
Non-urban			✓			✓	✓			✓	✓
Home visits								✓			
Conferences	✓	✓	✓	✓	✓	✓		✓			
Parents as volunteers							✓	✓			✓
Parents in advisory roles										✓	✓
Inclusion											
PPT meetings											
Multicultural	✓							✓	✓		✓
Teaching methods	✓		✓				✓	✓	✓	✓	✓
Identified disabilities											
Behavioral difficulties		✓	✓	✓	✓	✓					
Learning difficulties				✓				✓			
Other at-risk factors	✓	✓	✓	✓	✓	✓		✓	✓		
Legal issues			✓	✓	✓						

What's My Role?	My Mother Told Me . . .	Special Education	Support or Threat?	Which Problem Is Bigger?	Double Dilemma	Give Him an Inch . . .	High Hopes	The Case of Neglect	What's Best for Jamilah?	A Lack of Communication
12	13	14	15	16	17	18	19	20	21	22
✓	✓	✓			✓	✓	✓	✓		✓
	✓	✓	✓	✓	✓	✓	✓	✓	✓	✓
✓		✓		✓	✓	✓		✓		
			✓					✓	✓	
✓	✓	✓		✓	✓	✓	✓			✓
			✓	✓				✓		
✓		✓	✓	✓	✓	✓	✓		✓	✓
				✓			✓	✓		
	✓			✓	✓	✓	✓			✓
✓	✓	✓		✓	✓	✓	✓	✓	✓	✓
							✓	✓	✓	
✓	✓		✓			✓	✓		✓	✓
✓	✓			✓	✓	✓	✓		✓	✓
✓		✓								
✓		✓			✓			✓		
✓		✓	✓			✓		✓		✓
✓		✓	✓	✓	✓			✓		

Introduction

Imagine that you are a new teacher, teaching kindergarten for the first time. Mrs. Goodman, a parent of one of your students and a former teacher in this same school, has been volunteering every Tuesday in your class. Working side by side with her has become increasingly uncomfortable for you, as she often subtly criticizes your work and suggests changes she thinks you ought to make. Now you've heard that she has complained about your teaching to another teacher on the staff.

You started off on the right track, trying to encourage parent involvement by inviting Mrs. Goodman to volunteer in your classroom, but somehow things have gone awry. What do you do? What, in your education and experiences, do you draw on to help you negotiate this sticky situation? What has prepared you, so far, to foster positive relationships with parents? You may have taken courses in child development, curriculum, teaching methods, classroom management, and philosophy or history of education. But even if you have grappled with the theories—and are an expert at etiquette and managing people—how will you *apply* that knowledge?

There is an art to combining theory and practice. It's one thing to say, "Family involvement is good." It is entirely another to try, as a real life teacher, to nurture these complicated relationships. The beauty of this book's approach is that it ties theory to practice, forcing you to challenge your assumptions and grapple with the difficulties of implementing what we believe is sound policy.

THE IMPORTANCE OF PARENT INVOLVEMENT

> "It takes a whole village to raise a child."
> African proverb

During the past 30 years, research has shown that parental participation in schools improves students' learning (United States Department of Education, 1994). When parents get involved in their children's schools, students go to class more regularly, do their homework, make better grades, behave better at school, graduate, and go to college more frequently. (Henderson and Berla, 1994; Becher, 1984). In fact, the Goals 2000: Educate America Act

(P.L. 103–227) calls for schools to increase parent involvement as one of eight National Education Goals to build successful schools.

That said, what are the goals of parent involvement? What are we after? First, we recognize that a parent is the child's first teacher. By providing necessary knowledge and skills, educational professionals can support parents as they teach their children at every level. In turn, parents can support school efforts by valuing learning, instilling good work habits, monitoring homework, and keeping abreast of their children's progress.

Second, parent involvement encourages good communication between families and professionals. Mutual empathy is at the core of productive parent-teacher relationships and is crucial for resolving problems. Teachers and parents may start with different goals for children or face cultural and linguistic barriers. Through frequent open discussion, they can develop common aims and strategies for helping children to develop and learn. Such communication takes place in a variety of ways, including informal conversations, conferences, telephone calls, notes, and newsletters.

Third, parents can be resources in the classroom. Parents who volunteer even occasionally can provide additional hands, giving extra attention to individual children, creating learning materials, accompanying classes on field trips, and sharing interesting aspects of their own cultures. Moreover, their presence at school is a tangible sign to children that parents value education.

Fourth, parents can act in leadership capacities in schools. By serving on advisory committees or governance structures, parents can influence schoolwide policies and initiatives. Consequently, they will develop a real stake in school endeavors and will be more likely to ensure that these efforts meet with success.

A fifth goal of parent involvement is family support. In our complex world, many families need support in raising their children, so school professionals are now linking families to services available within the schools and communities. These resources often include psychological counseling, literacy programs, career training, parenting classes, health services, recreation programs, and other social services. Such support services help families create positive home environments for children's healthy development and academic learning. If parents already feel comfortable at school, they may be more likely to accept help within the school setting. They may also be more readily identifiable as needing support if they are regularly present at their children's school.

Dr. James Comer, founder and director of the School Development Program of the Yale Child Study Center, one of the most successful models in the United States for parent involvement, argues persuasively:

> When parents develop a strong, positive attachment to the school— and vice versa—a positive attachment of students to the staff and program of the school is more likely. Parents and school personnel are

then able to work together to motivate desirable academic and social performance among students. (Comer and Haynes, 1991, p. 274)

Let's say we agree with Dr. Comer. How are we going to hone our skills at working with *families*, not just with children? If we agree on a first principle that family involvement is a good thing for everybody, how do we nurture it and make it grow?

ADVANTAGES OF CASE STUDY

"Because wisdom can't be told."
Charles I. Gragg

Case studies have long been used to prepare lawyers, doctors, and executives. The case study approach used in these other educational encounters works well in teacher training. Here we'll follow the business school tradition of focusing on specific problems, because, like business, education is more often an art than a science (Schön, 1987).

Teachers routinely face confusing situations that they cannot solve simply by applying abstract rules or principles. The demands placed on a teacher change daily. Although you certainly need to master the theoretical knowledge in your field, there are no sure-fire, "right" answers that will see you through all the problems you will encounter. The case method encourages you to apply what you've learned, helping you to understand educational theory better and use it meaningfully. At its best, the case method leads you to see that your biggest assets in the classroom may be flexibility and adaptability, as well as a willingness to view conflicts from more than one vantage point.

Engaging in case study will sharpen your analytic and problem-solving skills. Daniel Schön, from the Massachusetts Institute of Technology, has spent years studying how teachers reflect on their professional practice. He observes that, when grappling with case problems, you will need to invent ways to frame the problems, reason about them, and design strategies that suit the particular circumstances at hand. By discussing your viewpoint with others, you will learn to examine your assumptions and theoretical understandings.

Case study will give you an opportunity to experience problems vicariously that teachers often confront. You'll put yourself in the position of the teacher in the case, imagining how you would face the knotty dilemma presented. Although there are many gratifying and even exhilarating times in teaching, teachers do face tough predicaments. Children may have trouble learning, parents may disagree with your recommendations and question your ability, and fellow professionals may be unsupportive. Cases can help to prepare you emotionally as well as intellectually for the often difficult realities of teaching (Kleinfeld, 1992).

Because case study is based on the belief that "wisdom can't be told" (Gragg, 1940), it forces you to learn actively. Cases engage you energetically in your own education. In classrooms where the case method is used, the stories present such compelling problems that the discussion often continues long after the period is over.

In short, the case method demonstrates the relevance of theory, develops your analytic and problem-solving skills, and encourages active learning. It familiarizes you with the real world of teaching, helping you to grow in your ability to "think like a teacher" (Kleinfeld, 1992).

HOW TO READ A CASE AND PREPARE FOR THE DISCUSSION

These cases are mystery stories, based on the experiences of real teachers. As you read, you should cast yourself in the role of the teacher, working to do the detective work needed to solve the case.

The cases begin with an incident. For example, you will encounter a child who begs a teacher not to call her father because he'll beat her if he learns of her misbehavior. Or you will read about a teacher who gets a telephone call from an angry father, complaining about his ex-wife's treatment of their child, a student in the class. What, you will wonder, caused these immediate problems to develop and how should the teacher handle them?

As you read on in each case, you will gain more background information, including descriptions of the community and school setting, the teacher, and the students and parents involved. One note: the term *Planning and Placement Team (PPT)* is used throughout this book. It may be called a *Child Study Team,* a *committee for the disabled,* or another term in various parts of the country. This team is responsible for assessing and planning an individualized education program for a student with special needs.

In some instances, you might wish you had more information about a particular concern. In others, you may feel that some of the information provided is not pertinent. But, in this way, the cases are like many of the situations teachers face in real life: we rarely have all of the information we would like and must make many decisions with incomplete or seemingly irrelevant information.

Knowing this, your responsibility is always (1) to analyze the case, and (2) to develop an action plan spelling out how the teacher should deal with the situation. Following are some guidelines.

Analyzing the Case

To analyze the case, you first need to determine the significant issues. Sometimes, the "presenting problem" is not as important as underlying issues. Like a detective, try to find subtle clues. Examine all the evidence closely and reflect on all of the options as you try to make sense out of the quandary.

Your analysis might be structured around the following questions:

1. *What has happened?* What events occurred? What are the facts?
2. *Why did this happen?* Was it because of the personalities of the individuals involved? What were the influences of the cultures of the family, the school, and the community? Was the style of the teacher a factor? Did the interaction of these elements contribute to creating a problem?
3. *How is the situation viewed by the various individuals?* Why might it be viewed from different perspectives? How has each individual responded to it so far? What is your own perspective on this matter?

As with any narrative, you will want to be aware of point of view. Who is narrating the story? What does the narrator have at stake? Are some voices missing? What happens when you try to give a voice to characters in the story who don't seem to be speaking up for themselves? Do you create a whole new story with different possible outcomes?

The discussion questions that follow each case will further guide you. To answer these, start with the facts, drawing upon specific evidence from the story itself. Then apply your theoretical knowledge. Consider relevant general information you've learned from other textbooks, reading, or your instructor's lectures. Also, you might have had personal experience with a similar issue that can provide you with insights or information. Your own stories may be as useful in deliberating the cases as the knowledge you've acquired in books.

Developing an Action Plan

Being a good teacher requires reflection and action. Teachers must be familiar with a variety of approaches. They must also know when and how to implement them. To develop strategies for a particular case, imagine yourself as the teacher. What would you do to resolve the predicament? What, if anything, would you have the other characters do? At first, think broadly and try to brainstorm about as many alternative ways to deal with the dilemma as possible. Be flexible. Then, evaluate your options and consider whether they are:

1. Consistent: Do the recommendations for action flow from your analysis in a logical and consistent way?
2. Feasible: Can the recommendations be carried out within the context described? For example, are they realistic if the teacher has limited time or the school's budget is being cut back?
3. Operational: Are the recommendations clear enough and specific enough so that the teacher can follow them? (Greenwood and Parkay, 1989)

Based on your conclusions, refine your action plan and try to anticipate why others may disagree with you. You should be prepared to explain and defend your approach in the class discussion.

DISCUSSING THE CASE IN CLASS

Because the cases present complicated teaching problems, several solutions may be possible, although some may seem better than others. Like teaching itself, there is no one right solution, much less an easy answer.

Your instructor will encourage everyone to participate in the discussion, so that a variety of viewpoints are represented. At times, your teacher may play devil's advocate to broaden your thinking, drawing out other perspectives. We tend to look at issues from our own personal fixes, and no one person is likely to consider all of the possibilities. The cases are designed to challenge your thinking and to help you to come to deeper understanding through a shared learning process.

Be ready for a lively debate. Present your analysis and your plan reasonably and logically, with appropriate supporting evidence. Listen carefully to others' positions. Try to identify the strengths and weaknesses in their arguments and respectfully express your disagreements. Be open to new ideas and don't be surprised if you begin to change your mind about your own solution. This is part of the important process of developing a reflective stance.

Thinking aloud about these cases will sharpen your awareness of the complexity and richness of parental involvement in schools. It will heighten your sensitivity to parents' concerns and develop your skill in working collaboratively with parents.

References

Becher, R. 1984. *Parent involvement: A review of research and principles of successful practice*. Washington, DC: National Institute of Education.

Comer, J. P., and N. M. Haynes. 1991. Parent involvement in schools: An ecological approach. *Elementary School Journal* 91 (3): 271–277.

Gragg, C. I. 1940. *Because wisdom can't be told*. Boston: Harvard Business School.

Greenwood, G. E., and F. W. Parkay. 1989. *Case studies for teacher decision making*. New York: Random House.

Henderson, A. T., and N. Berla. 1994. *A new generation of evidence: The family is critical to student achievement*. Washington, DC: National Committee for Citizens in Education.

Kleinfeld, J. 1992. Learning to think like a teacher: The study of cases. In J. H. Shulman, ed., *Case methods in teacher education*, pp. 33–49. New York: Teachers College Press.

Schön, D. 1987. *Educating the reflective practitioner*. San Francisco: Jossey-Bass.

United States Department of Education. 1994. *Strong families: Strong schools*. Washington, DC: U.S. Department of Education.

A Conflict of Interest

Day-care teacher:	Rita Leary
Day-care director:	Evelyn Sendak
Student:	José Cruz
Parents:	Theresa and Adriano Cruz

The children were following their daily routine at the day-care center on a breezy October day. It was midmorning, and the clean-up period after the free play time had just ended. As the children finished picking up blocks or putting away puzzles, they went to the bathroom and washed their hands to get ready for snack. After snack, the group would go outside.

José listlessly dropped a few Lego pieces into the bucket. Then, as usual, he seated himself stiffly on a chair and watched the other children in stony silence. Once again, he refused to go into the bathroom. Rita Leary, the head teacher, observed him from across the room and tried to think of a new way to handle this situation. She knew that, in all likelihood, José would wet his pants later in the day.

THE SCHOOL AND COMMUNITY

The day-care center was affiliated with the hospital in the city of Newmark. The director of the center, Evelyn Sendak, considered herself lucky to run a developmentally appropriate program that was well staffed and well equipped. There were two infant-toddler groups, one group for three-year-olds, and one group for four-year-olds. The center was housed in a once-elegant brick Victorian house. Although the building had been renovated to meet day-care requirements, there was still a homey feel about it.

José was in a group of eighteen three-year-olds with three well-trained teachers. The children at the center were from the hospital community and included children of the medical personnel, administrators, clerical staff, and physical plant workers. They were from varied socioeconomic and ethnic backgrounds, but José was the only child born in the Philippines.

Rita Leary had been teaching for seven years. She had a degree in early childhood education and originally thought she'd like to work with school-age children. However, she did her student teaching in an excellent preschool program, loved the experience, and decided to stay with that age level. She was an ample, gentle woman, and children often liked to curl up in her large, consoling lap.

THE CHILD AND THE FAMILY

Three-year-old José Cruz lived with his parents, his grandparents, and his one-year-old sister. His parents had immigrated to the United States two years earlier from the Philippines, and his grandparents had arrived the following year. Both of José's parents worked as lab technicians at the hospital. José's grandparents, who lived with the Cruzes, helped with the care of José and his one-year-old sister while their parents were working.

The Cruzes spoke Tagalog at home, and José came to day care with little knowledge of English. In addition, Mrs. Cruz explained to the teachers that José had rarely played with children other than his sister. The teachers weren't sure why this was the case but presumed that there were not many young children in the neighborhood. Not surprisingly, José started the year with considerable apprehension. He was enrolled in a half-day program. Rita vividly remembered the small, solemn boy refusing to leave his mother's side the entire first day.

SEPARATION

The center staff knew that some distress over separation from parents was common for many children just starting day care. Therefore, they encouraged parents to introduce their children to the program gradually. Mr. and Mrs. Cruz had alternately taken time off from work during José's first week of school, initially spending whole mornings and then partial mornings with him. Both his parents and teachers hoped to acclimate him to his new surroundings, teachers, and playmates before he had to adjust to separation from his family.

The Cruzes carefully followed the teachers' guidelines for handling the separation. When it was time for them to leave each morning, they gave José a warm hug, said good-bye firmly, and then, despite his protests, left without hesitation. Although this was painful both for José and for them, Mr. and Mrs. Cruz trusted the teachers' advice.

Despite this planned gradual separation, José wept for long periods each morning and refused to play or interact with the other children. And, although he had used the bathroom during the first week of day care, he now refused to use it.

At Rita's suggestion, his parents had written him a note, with their photograph attached, to keep in his pocket as a reminder of them. The small boy was racked with silent sobs when he looked longingly at the picture—a heartbreaking sight to the teachers. Rita tried to comfort him.

His only consolation seemed to be the relationship he was developing with Rita. He clung to her, clenching her hand. He became her shadow as she supervised children in the block area, the sand table, or at snack time. Although her interactions with other children were sometimes restricted by this hand-holding, from experience Rita knew that children often first developed an attachment to one teacher. She hoped that this trusting relationship would be a bridge to comfortable relations with other teachers and children.

JOSÉ'S GRANDPARENTS

After the first week, José's grandparents brought him to and from day care. José sometimes arrived late, and, if he didn't want to stay, his grandparents would take him right back home. At times, José never even came.

One morning, José insisted that his grandmother stay with him at day care and play for awhile. They built with blocks. When his grandmother accidentally knocked down the tower, José yelled at her. Looking embarrassed, she began to rebuild the structure by herself.

Rita noticed a marked difference in the way that José's parents and grandparents interacted with him. She remembered a discussion she had had with the Filipino parent of a former student. According to that mother, parents' behavior toward young children in the traditional Philippines might seem indulgent to some Americans. Rita thought perhaps José's parents were adopting the ways of their new American culture, while his grandparents were adhering to older customs. Was José caught in the middle?

A TIME OF ADJUSTMENT

During September and early October, the teachers worked to help José grow more comfortable. They spent hours discussing ways to reduce José's dependence on Rita and to get him to use the bathroom. They tried to ease the transition in culture and the language barrier by learning some Tagalog words and playing simple language games with José. They even learned a few Filipino songs and encouraged José and the other children to sing with them. They also nurtured his slowly developing relationship with another child, Jeffrey.

Although the teachers accepted José's need to be close to Rita, they all felt that it was important to wean him gradually from this dependence and move him beyond a single relationship. So, for example, they sometimes assigned him to work with other teachers during an activity time. Rita was consistently caring and supportive of José, but she was relieved to have occasional breaks.

José gradually became more a part of the group, yet his refusal to use the bathroom continued. Rita tried to take him by the hand and gently lead him into the bathroom, during quiet times when no other children would bustle in. But José planted his feet firmly on the floor, refusing to budge.

Moreover, there were other resistant behaviors. José seemed to avoid cleanup in a passive way, taking a long time to put away even a few blocks. Once, on a particularly blustery day, he stubbornly refused to wear his coat. Another time, he ran into the school building during outdoor play when everyone else was on the playground.

The teachers ordinarily chatted with parents at drop off and pick up times, filling them in on their child's ups and downs during the day. But it was difficult for them to communicate with José's grandparents because they knew little English. Their major transaction seemed to be an exchange of a plastic bag with wet underpants at the end of the day and clean, dry underpants in the morning. José's grandparents didn't appear the least disconcerted, and Rita wondered whether his parents knew the extent of the problem.

The Cruzes worked long hours, and Rita had not seen them since the first week of school. They lived in a suburb about a half hour away, and they had not returned to the city to go to the center's open house for parents in mid-September. Once, Rita had called them to discuss the situation, but communication over the telephone was difficult because they did not speak English well.

WHAT NEXT?

Rita had been sharing her concerns about José with Evelyn, the center's director. Both Rita and Evelyn understood that children's adjustment to day care often takes time, so they hadn't wanted to overreact to José's behavior. Now, it was late October, and they saw little improvement. José still clung to Rita, interacted minimally with other children, and wet his pants each day.

Although the first parent-teacher conferences were normally held in late November, both Evelyn and Rita felt that it was time to confer with José's parents. For a variety of reasons, they faced the conference with apprehension. It was always difficult to express concerns about a child to a parent. But, in this case, it would be even harder because of language differences. Furthermore, there was the issue of the possible contrast in parenting styles between José's parents and grandparents. Should Rita raise this issue? She didn't want to create conflict within the family. José's parents clearly needed his grandparents' help and support. And Rita didn't want to imply disrespect for another culture's traditions.

Discussion Questions

1. What problem(s) is Rita facing? How did this situation develop?
2. What underlying issues are involved?
3. How do you think this situation appears from the perspective of Rita? José? Mr. and Mrs. Cruz? José's grandparents? The other children?
4. What steps has the school already taken to try to deal with the problem(s)?
   - How appropriate was the school's approach to dealing with children's separation problems?
   - What other strategies might Rita and the other teachers have tried?
5. If you were Rita, what would you do at this point?
   - Is there a need for Rita or the Cruzes to consult with other specialists, such as a pediatrician? Why or why not? With whom?
6. Is there a role for a multicultural curriculum here? If not, why not? If so, what experiences might be helpful?
7. Is a conference even necessary at this point? Why or why not?
   - If a conference is held, how should it be handled?
   - Who should be present and why? Evelyn? José's grandparents? Others?
   - What should Rita say to or ask the Cruzes?
   - How might the participants deal with the differences in language?
8. Would it be helpful to seek information from a family of similar background? Why or why not?

Suggested Activities

1. Role-play a parent-teacher conference based on the classes' discussion. What are the concerns of the various participants? What strategies might be used to address these concerns?
2. Interview a teacher who is working with a child who has recently immigrated. Did the child have any problems adjusting? If so, what has the teacher done to help the child adjust? Has the teacher worked with the child's parents and, if so, how? How is the situation different from or similar to José's? Have there been school-based efforts to work with immigrant families and, if so, what?
3. Review multicultural curricula to identify activities or ideas that might have been helpful to the teachers, José, and his family in this situation.

The Butterfly

CHARACTERS

Kindergarten teacher:	Alicia Garcia
Student:	Claudia Sturman
Parents:	Mr. and Dr. Sturman

"I just don't . . . I just don't . . . I just don't think this story makes sense. How could . . . how could . . . how could a caterpillar that eats people's food have the normal life cycle of a butterfly? It's confusing," commented Claudia. Alicia Garcia and the kindergarten children were dumbstruck. Claudia's severe stuttering often preceded a comment that astonished her teacher and befuddled the children. Wasn't *The Very Hungry Caterpillar* just a wonderful fantasy?

SCHOOL AND COMMUNITY

Lincoln Elementary School was located in Centerville, a small city in the middle of the state. Families from a range of socioeconomic groups lived there. In addition to a few high-rise apartment buildings in mid-town, there were sections of sleek condominiums, gracious colonial homes on shady lots, and tracts of more modest split-level houses.

Lincoln was built five years earlier with the goal of racially balancing the city's schools. Children who lived in the school's neighborhood were guaranteed a place. Children from outside the district could apply and were then selected through a lottery system. The school's special appeal was its computer-based curriculum, and parents vied for their children to attend. The five computers in every classroom were in constant use.

Lincoln had about 300 students. There were four half-day kindergartens, two transitional classrooms, four first grades, and four second grades. Teachers appreciated the small class size and sought to increase the adult-child ratio further by encouraging parents to volunteer in their classrooms. Parent involvement was an aspect of the school that both teachers and parents valued.

Alicia Garcia, a stocky woman with a halo of curly red hair, had been teaching for ten years, the last three in a kindergarten. Her booming voice resonated through the classroom. She had high expectations for the nineteen children, and her ready smile was quickly replaced by a frown when she was dissatisfied with their behavior or performance. Though she might at times reprimand children gruffly, she also showed gentle understanding.

The learning centers in her classroom included an art area, block area, science table, reading corner, dramatic play area, and, naturally, the computer center. However, most of the children's day was spent participating in relatively structured activities to ensure that before moving on to first grade, they knew letter names and sounds, had basic counting skills, and could recognize colors. For about a half hour a day, the children had "choice time" when they could work in the learning centers. Alicia felt that at least some time to play was crucial for healthy development. While most of the children enjoyed talking with Alicia and showing her their artistic efforts or other work, Claudia Sturman did not.

THE CHILD AND THE FAMILY

Claudia was five and a half years old. She had large, intense brown eyes and dark straight hair that draped gently on her shoulders. She was of average height and weight. Her voice was soft, and Alicia and the children sometimes had to strain to hear her.

In fact, her entire demeanor was reticent. She seemed to isolate herself from the rest of the group. During the morning exercises, she carefully created a separate space for herself outside of the circle. She seemed distressed when the other children nudged or bumped into her, even by accident. She rarely raised her hand to ask questions or offer a comment. Nor did she take pride in being a "good helper," volunteering for tasks like watering the plants or getting the milk for snack like the other children. At times, her gloomy expressions made her look very sad.

Claudia was the oldest of three children in her family. Her father was a journalist and her mother was a dentist. Her mother tried to limit her practice to twenty-five hours a week, but there always seemed to be dental emergencies that made extra demands on her.

CLAUDIA'S SELF-EXPRESSION

During choice time, Claudia played alone in the art area. There, she appeared to lose herself in her drawing and became animated. She laughed, smiled, and carried on quiet conversations with herself. Alicia couldn't hear these well enough to determine whether she was stuttering then.

Her art was far more sophisticated than that of the typical five-year-old. She once drew a picture of herself at the easel, as viewed from behind. Her drawing of a jungle scene contained several different kinds of animals and showed a sense of perspective. A cheetah peeking around a tree was only partially visible, and Claudia explained to Alicia that you couldn't see the middle of his body because it was behind the tree. Alicia was impressed by her level of abstract understanding.

Although Claudia communicated well through her art, she had difficulty expressing herself verbally. She often stuttered, not on the initial sound of a word, but generally by repeating whole words or phrases several times. For example, she might say, "I want to . . . I want to . . . I want to . . ." before completing her sentence. Claudia rarely volunteered to speak during group activities. When Alicia called on her to ask her a question, she spoke softly and stuttered. She often stuffed her fingers in her mouth, which seemed to be a nervous habit. Alicia and the children patiently waited for Claudia to compose herself and continue.

However, Claudia's vocabulary was advanced for her age. Alicia had observed Dr. Sturman talking to her as if she were an adult and speculated that this might have been a source of Claudia's extensive vocabulary.

PARENT-TEACHER CONFERENCES

Since early in the year, Alicia had felt some concern about Claudia's tendency to isolate herself and to avoid talking. Kindergarten is an important year in the growth of a child's social skills, and Claudia did not seem to be developing these. At the first parent-teacher conference in November, Alicia had gently broached these issues with the Sturmans. Although she was not ready to recommend an assessment for special services, she wanted to tune Claudia's parents in to her concerns and prepare them for the possible need for future action. She still hoped that, in time, Claudia would grow more comfortable in the classroom and this would alleviate her difficulties.

As she did with all the parents, Alicia encouraged the Sturmans to visit the classroom. She felt that it was useful for parents to see their own child among the other children, to get a sense of similarities and differences in development. She also felt that Claudia might feel supported or reassured by her parents' presence. Although they wanted to come, it was difficult with younger children in the family and with their busy work schedules.

By the February conference with the Sturmans, Alicia had not observed any progress in Claudia's social development. Academically, she was progressing well and readily mastered and even surpassed kindergarten-level skills and concepts. But she was still a loner. The other children were not mean to Claudia; they simply ignored her. Alicia had paired Claudia a few times with another girl in the art area, but the relationship didn't seem to take.

Whenever Claudia spoke, Alicia praised her comments to encourage her participation further. But this didn't help either. She wasn't even sure that this was a helpful strategy. Perhaps she should draw as little attention to Claudia as possible.

At the conference, Alicia described her observations of Claudia. She emphasized Claudia's strengths but also expressed her concerns. She thought that Claudia was embarrassed by her stutter and that she might well need special services to help her. When Alicia recommended that Claudia be referred to the speech-language pathologist for an evaluation, Mr. and Dr. Sturman flatly rejected this suggestion.

"I really don't think that's necessary. Claudia's shy like I was as a child. I'm sure she'll grow out of it, just as I did," Dr. Sturman said. "She doesn't have any trouble playing with her brothers," added Mr. Sturman.

"She's very bright and we think her stuttering is related to her high intelligence," Dr. Sturman continued. "I've noticed that she stutters when she's grappling with sophisticated concepts and struggling to articulate them. It can happen anywhere—at school, at home, in the grocery store. It seems like her level of understanding surpasses her ability to express her ideas, so she gets frustrated. We really think that as she grows older, her language skills will catch up with her intellectual ability, and then the stuttering will naturally stop."

Mr. Sturman said, "We appreciate your work with Claudia in the classroom. But if you recommend her for special services, she might feel stigmatized in some way and grow even more self-conscious."

Alicia thanked the Sturmans for sharing their perspective with her; they had certainly given her food for thought. She promised to keep in touch, and the conference ended on an amicable note.

HOW TO PROCEED

It was now March, a month later, and there was still little change in Claudia's social development or speech problem since the beginning of the year. Alicia had to begin to plan the children's placements for next year. While Claudia was quite intelligent, she was socially immature; she might benefit from the transition class rather than going straight on to first grade. This class had approximately eight children in it, and Claudia would receive more attention from the teacher. Also, it might be easier for her to develop friendships and to speak more comfortably in a smaller group. Alicia still felt that Claudia should be evaluated for speech therapy.

She sensed that the Sturmans would be opposed to the transition class. Could she convince them that this would help Claudia develop necessary skills and would not simply hold her back? She herself wasn't absolutely confident that this was the right step. The Sturmans' arguments about their daughter seemed to make sense, she mused, as she remembered Claudia's perceptive comment about the life cycle of a butterfly. Was this simply a maturational problem? Maybe Claudia would experience a natural transformation, like a butterfly.

She knew that she would have to make placement recommendations in the next few weeks. What should she do?

Discussion Questions

1. What problem(s) does Alicia face?
2. What underlying issues are involved in this case?
3. Review the actions Alicia has already taken to deal with the problem(s). How effective do you feel these steps have been?
   - Do you think Alicia should have pressed harder for Claudia to be assessed for possible speech therapy? Please explain.
4. How sound do you feel the Sturmans' perspectives are?
5. Should Alicia have taken any other steps?
   - Is there a role for other staff in the school? If so, who and what role?
6. What should Alicia do now?
   - Given your present knowledge, do you feel that Claudia should be placed in a transition class next year?
   - Consider again the Sturman's comments about their daughter in light of this.
7. What could Alicia do now to enlist the Sturmans' support for whatever recommendation she might make about Claudia?

Suggested Activities

1. Role-play another conference between Alicia and the Sturmans at which Alicia makes a recommendation for Claudia's placement for next year. Work in trios and alternate the roles of teacher and parents. What are the concerns of each? Which concerns are similar and which are different?
2. Write a research paper on stuttering. What are the possible causes? What are the differences between typical and atypical nonfluency? What strategies are recommended for helping a student who stutters? Which of these might be implemented in a regular classroom? What strategies might teachers recommend for parents to try at home?
3. Interview a speech-language pathologist in a school to find out whether she or he could take informal steps to assess and, if necessary, help Claudia, without a formal assessment. If so, what might those be? What recommendations might the speech-language pathologist make to Claudia's parents?
4. Review the research literature to determine current thinking in education about transition classes. Write a paper exploring this issue.

He'll Beat Me!

CHARACTERS

Second-grade teacher:	Maureen Quinn
Student:	Leslie Kurtz
Parents:	Joseph and Adele Kurtz

Maureen Quinn, a second-grade teacher, was helping some children with their journal work when she heard a scream from the far corner of the room. In her haste to get to the bathroom, Leslie Kurtz had rammed into another child and knocked her over. The child was crying indignantly, and Leslie stood near her with a sullen look on her face, as if waiting to be reprimanded once again.

THE SCHOOL, COMMUNITY, AND TEACHER

Lamberton was a suburban community of approximately 50,000. The residents were primarily middle class and worked in the town's retail businesses, light industries, banks, and insurance companies. A few low-income neighborhoods dotted the shoreline. Because of a recent recession, there had been an increase in the area's unemployment. Some factories had moved south, and property values had declined. The jai alai fronton, another source of revenue, was suffering from competition from a large gambling casino that had opened an hour away.

High Slope Elementary School had about 500 children in its kindergarten through fifth grades, and it housed all of the town's special education programs. As a result, the school staff had a full-time nurse and several special education professionals. The school and district had supported inclusive education for the past few years, and children with special needs were included in the regular classes as much as possible.

Maureen Quinn had taught at High Slope for fifteen years, the last eight teaching second grade. A tall, thin woman, she moved around the classroom energetically. She had high expectations for both herself and the children, and she was often heard remarking to a child, "You can do it!" She kept herself up to date on curriculum and methodology and enjoyed trying out new ideas. For example, the children were just completing their own Big Book, which they had composed and were typing on the computer.

A few years ago, Maureen had introduced an approach to discipline in her classroom that she felt generally worked well. It emphasized consistently setting clear limits, following through on problem behavior, and providing positive consequences for appropriate behavior. To warn a child of a misbehavior, Maureen wrote her name on the board. For a second misbehavior, the child received a check by her name and was denied a choice of learning centers during the activity time. For a third misbehavior, the child received a second check by her name and the child's parent was called. Maureen found that this system, if consistently followed, worked well to make children more conscious of their behavior and helped them begin to take responsibility for it. Indeed, she rarely had to call a parent.

THE CHILD AND THE FAMILY

While Leslie Kurtz managed reasonably well academically, Maureen was concerned about her social development. Leslie was larger than most of the other girls and barreled her way around the room, often bumping into the other children or knocking their papers off their desks.

When a group of children was playing, Leslie seemed unsure how to join them. She would talk loudly or push her way into the center of the group. As a result, the other children had begun to shun her. Although Maureen tried to intervene and to teach Leslie more effective social skills, she had not been successful. In fact, Leslie's behavior seemed to be getting worse.

Leslie lived with her parents and three older brothers. Her father had been a machinist in a small shop that had closed, so he had been unemployed for two months, since early December. In order to help the family make ends meet, Mrs. Kurtz had taken a job as a clerk on the second shift in a convenience store. Mr. Kurtz took care of the children after school, fed them dinner, helped them with their homework, and got them to bed. Recently, when Mr. Kurtz picked Leslie up from school, Maureen thought she smelled alcohol on his breath.

Mrs. Kurtz had attended the first parent-teacher conference in November. Maureen described Leslie's progress in the academic areas and then gently raised the issue of Leslie's social skills. Mrs. Kurtz explained that their home was isolated from other houses in the neighborhood and there were no children Leslie's age nearby. Leslie tended to play with her brothers, who were nine, 11 and 12 years old. Mrs. Kurtz guessed that Leslie had just adopted their rambunctious style of play.

Maureen suggested that Mrs. Kurtz try to invite a child from Leslie's class over after school once in a while to help her to develop some relationships among her peers. It was soon after this conference that Mr. Kurtz lost his job and things had turned topsy-turvy for the family.

THE SITUATION DETERIORATES

There had been several incidents in the last weeks that alarmed Maureen. The school had a new adventure playground that had been funded and constructed through the efforts of the parent-teacher organization. The children loved to climb the turrets of this wooden structure, swing on its tire swing, and balance across its wobbly chain bridge. During recess, three girls lined up on the platform waiting their turns to cross the bridge, Leslie among them. When Stephanie seemed to be taking too long to cross, Leslie angrily shouted at her to hurry up. Then she jumped onto the bridge herself, causing Stephanie to lose her balance and fall off. Although the bridge was only a few feet off the ground, Stephanie was clearly shaken. She had skinned her knee and was crying when Maureen got to the scene. Maureen calmly but firmly reminded Leslie of the rules and told her to sit on a bench on the sidelines for five minutes to cool off.

A few days later, Leslie yelled "Shut up!" at Sam, another child. Maureen intervened to help Leslie and Sam resolve their dispute. She wrote Leslie's name on the board as a warning about her behavior.

An hour later, the children were drawing pictures for a book they were making. Leslie and three other children were sharing two boxes of crayons. Leslie wanted the green crayon to color some trees, but another child was using it. She waited for a minute or two and then lunged for the crayon. Once she had it, she furiously slashed dark green marks across the other child's paper.

At this point, Maureen admonished Leslie. She removed her from the table and gave her another assignment; then she put a check after her name. Now Leslie would have to work on her drawing during the activity time, instead of having a choice of activities.

As the day continued, Maureen sensed that the tension was building in Leslie. During afternoon story time, she asked Leslie to sit next to her, and she put her hand on the child's shoulder. Leslie seemed soothed by the story and comforted by contact with her teacher.

For the day's final activity, Maureen gave the children a worksheet. They were to cut out the pictures and accompanying text and rearrange them in proper chronological sequence. As she was working with one of the students, Sam called out, "Mrs. Quinn!" She looked over and saw Leslie taunting Sam and brandishing the scissors in his face. Maureen rushed over and took the scissors from Leslie. She then took the child's hand and led her to the board. "I can't let you hurt other children," she stated firmly and explained that she would have to call Leslie's mother and father. As she marked the second check on the board, Leslie began to flail her arms and cried, "Don't do that! Don't! He'll beat me!"

Discussion Questions

1. What are the underlying issues in this situation?
2. What do you think of how Maureen handled the situation so far? What, if anything, would you have done differently?
3. What steps should Mrs. Quinn take now?
   - How should Maureen respond to Leslie after her comment about her father beating her?
   - Is this a case of child abuse? If so, what are Maureen's legal responsibilities?
   - Should she hold a conference with Leslie's parents? If so, what should she say?
   - At this point, what other professionals in the school system might Maureen call on for assistance?
4. What else can Maureen do to help Leslie and her family?
   - How might stresses on the family be related to Leslie's difficulties?
   - Are there likely to be other agencies in the community that might help them? If so, which ones and how? Is it an appropriate role for a teacher to connect parents to those resources? If so, how might this be done?
   - Should Maureen change her strategies with Leslie in the classroom?

Suggested Activities

1. Investigate and write a report on a school district's policies and procedures for identifying and reporting suspected child abuse. What are the requirements of the state law and penalties for not reporting? What are the responsibilities of the teacher, other school professionals such as the social worker or nurse, and the principal? What agencies work with the school on this issue?
2. Role-play a conference after the incident in which Leslie says her father will beat her. Determine who should be present at the conference: Maureen? Mrs. Kurtz? Mr. Kurtz? The principal? Other school personnel? Try to reflect possible perspectives of each of the characters as you role-play the conference.
3. How might you help parents learn strategies for effective parenting? Locate agencies in the community that offer resources. In a written report, describe these services and develop a plan to disseminate this information to parents (newsletter, bulletin board, conference, and so on).
4. Research the topic of young children and behavioral disorders. What are possible causes? What classroom interventions are recommended? Write a paper discussing your findings.

A Family Matter

CHARACTERS

Second-grade teacher:	Mary Robles
School social worker:	Ellen Mark
Student:	Jocelyn Daniels
Grandmother:	Bessie Daniels
Aunt:	Virginia Daniels

It was a gorgeous mid-October day, and Mary Robles had decided to take her second graders out for a longer play time. She wanted to take advantage of what would probably be one of the last balmy days before winter set in. The children had been working hard and deserved a break. Moreover, the parents had finally finished their two year fund-raising effort to buy a climbing structure, which had just been installed on the playground. A relatively modest piece of equipment, it seemed like a castle to the children, who had been used to only a bare field and an old metal swing set.

As she was standing near the climber, chatting with one of the children, Mary heard a scream. Looking up, she saw Jocelyn pushing Ruth closer and closer to the edge of the four-foot-high platform of the climber. She rushed to that side of the climber and raised her hand protectively to prevent a fall.

"Jocelyn, get down here immediately!" she insisted. "Are you okay, Ruth?" she asked. "You come down, too."

When both girls had climbed down, she talked to them about the incident. Ruth was clearly shaken and seemed leery of even getting near Jocelyn to talk.

"Jocelyn, you know pushing is dangerous! What happened?" Mary asked.

"She called me names," Jocelyn retorted loudly. Mary then turned to Ruth to confirm this.

Looking stunned, Ruth responded quietly but firmly, "I did not."

Although Mary had not seen the incident, she suspected that Jocelyn had, indeed, pushed Ruth without provocation. Jocelyn seemed to lash out for no reason at all and had been getting into conflicts with different children. Mary firmly told Jocelyn that she would need to have a time-out in a far corner of the playground.

But this, Mary knew, was only a temporary solution and wouldn't change Jocelyn's behavior. She resolved to talk with Jocelyn's grandmother again when she picked her up this afternoon.

THE SCHOOL, COMMUNITY, AND TEACHER

The mid-sized city of Fitchburg had a population of about 150,000, approximately 30 percent white, 30 percent African-American, and 40 percent Hispanic. The city had several colleges and universities, as well as the distinction of being the birthplace of the founder of a famous circus, whose statue stood in the main park.

Fitchburg's factories once hummed busily, producing machine tools, brass products, and electrical equipment for the entire Eastern seaboard. There had also been a large garment industry. Although some factories remained open, most had closed and the economy had changed to a service base.

Benton Road School was a public magnet school with about 500 students in kindergarten through fourth grade. The curriculum emphasized developmentally based instruction. In the lower grades, children studied a key theme, and subject areas were integrated within this theme as much as possible.

Because of the dedication of the teachers and the innovative approach to instruction, the school attracted children from throughout the city, and parents had to apply to the program. A lottery was held to determine which children could attend. It was carefully designed to ensure that there was a balance of ethnicity, gender, and family income level in the school's population. The teaching staff was also balanced racially and ethnically.

Since its founding 25 years earlier, parents had a central role at Benton Road School. Many of the parents who helped to start the school were activists, community organizers, and veterans of the civil rights movement. They believed that it was important to empower individuals to take charge of their own institutions, and parent involvement had been a clearly articulated element of Benton Road's mission from the beginning.

At this point, the parents continued to be highly involved in their children's education. They helped them with homework. They volunteered in classrooms, tutoring children, carrying out projects, and chaperoning field trips. They also served on school committees in an advisory capacity.

The school was housed in what had been an old run-down building, which teachers and parents transformed into an appealing setting by dint of sheer energy and enthusiasm. The building's bright interior was a marked contrast to its decaying neighborhood. It was not uncommon to find used hypodermic needles and broken liquor bottles on the sidewalks leading to the school.

This was Mary Robles's first year of teaching. Having graduated from one of the colleges in the city, she was hired at Benton Road School after her successful student teaching experience there. (These had been a rare opening because of a maternity leave at the school.) She had worked hard in college and was excited about trying out the new ideas she had learned in her teacher training program.

She was also a little scared. Student teaching had gone fine, but she always knew she had the reassuring backup of her master teacher. Now the responsibility for the class was hers. She had really been applying herself, planning lessons and developing materials, and, so far, thank goodness, things seemed to be going reasonably smoothly.

Except for the problem with Jocelyn . . .

There were 25 children in her class, which was fairly evenly divided between boys and girls. One-third of the children received free breakfasts and lunches. Approximately half of the class came from two-parent families. Three students were being raised by their grandparents, and the remainder lived in single-parent families.

Mary had tried to make the room a safe, inviting setting for the children. The walls were decorated with collages that the children had made and with posters about children's books. Learning centers lined the sides of the room. The desks were grouped to make tables of four, so children could work together and support each other.

Mary had set aside a small area of the classroom as a calm-down place. Children who felt the need to compose themselves sometimes went there voluntarily. At other times, when a child was disruptive or out of control, Mary would place him or her there for five minutes.

Although the principal was supportive of teachers in other ways, she rarely got involved in disciplinary issues. She was busy with the overall management of the school and felt that discipline was essentially the responsibility of the teachers. Occasionally, Mary asked her former master teacher for advice, but she didn't want to be a bother or to appear dependent.

THE CHILD AND FAMILY

Jocelyn Daniels, who was seven years old, lived with her four-year-old brother, her grandmother, and her aunt. Her mother had lost custody of the two children because of persistent drug abuse. When the family became homeless two years ago, the children went to live with their grandmother and aunt in Bessie Daniels's modest but well-kept house.

The school social worker, Ellen Mark, had been apprised of this situation by a social worker from the Child Welfare Bureau. Sharing the information with Mary, Ellen explained that Jocelyn's mother occasionally visited the children. It was not an easy relationship; the children were alternately loving and rejecting towards her. No information was available about Jocelyn's father.

Every day, Bessie Daniels walked her granddaughter to school and picked her up in the afternoon, so Mary frequently saw her. She was a plump woman in her late fifties, but she looked much older. Her hair was already white, and her face was lined with wrinkles. She trudged slowly, trying to keep a rein on her two energetic grandchildren.

When the school grounds came in sight, Jocelyn often twisted free of her grandmother's grasp and raced ahead. Many mornings while on yard duty Mary would hear Mrs. Daniels calling Jocelyn to come back and hold her hand, but the child simply ran on, ignoring her grandmother.

Jocelyn was having difficulty at school. She was frequently disruptive. During the circle time, she chatted with or poked the other children. A few times, she stood up in front of another child, who then couldn't see Mary. When the other child complained, Jocelyn stared at Mary with her arms crossed and a belligerent look on her face. She refused to move until Mary took her hand and personally walked her to the calm-down area.

Jocelyn rarely completed her work. When it was time to collect papers, she often had written only her name. Mary tried to give her some individual attention, during journal writing time, for example. But Mary had twenty-four other children to teach and as soon as she left Jocelyn's side, Jocelyn stopped working. Sometimes she started writing on other children's papers, as if to attract attention. When Mary confronted Jocelyn, she'd simply smile smugly at her. Mary wondered if her disruptive behavior was caused by a lack of understanding of the work.

Mary had spoken to Mrs. Daniels several times about Jocelyn's difficulties. Mrs. Daniels simply nodded in acknowledgment and said to Jocelyn, "You shouldn't do that." Jocelyn did not respond. Mary did not know whether Mrs. Daniels was able to help Jocelyn much at home. It seemed the grandmother might have her hands full with the two young children.

THE CONFERENCE

By mid-November, at the time of the first report card conference, Mary was very concerned about Jocelyn. As the class work became more difficult, Jocelyn had grown more disruptive and she was having great difficulty with reading. Although she recognized letters and had a small sight vocabulary, she still did not know many vowel and consonant sounds. While several of the other children zoomed along in the easy readers, Jocelyn struggled to decode new vocabulary.

Parents were asked to come to school for conferences to receive their children's first report card. The 15-minute conferences were held in the early morning, afternoon, and early evening one day, and during the early morning and late afternoon on two other days. Children received grades of Excellent, Satisfactory, Needs Improvement, or Unsatisfactory.

Jocelyn's first report card was not good. Although her grades in the specials—such as gym, music, and art—were satisfactory, her reading skills and the other academic areas needed improvement. She also received grades of unsatisfactory in the areas of social development, such as following school rules and respecting other's property.

Jocelyn's grandmother arrived at five o'clock for the conference. Since Mary had often communicated with her, she was already aware of how her granddaughter was doing. However, Mary showed her some samples of Jocelyn's work and tried to explain that Jocelyn was accomplishing very little during the course of most days. Mrs. Daniels just sat and listened; occasionally she nodded. Mary suggested ways that Mrs. Daniels might help Jocelyn at home, by reading to her, for example, and playing simple number games. Mrs. Daniels responded wearily, "I'll do what I can." After the grandmother departed, Mary wondered how she was going to get Jocelyn the help she needed.

At eight o'clock, Mary was gathering together her papers and marking book to get ready to leave. (The principal had established a school policy that all staff were to leave the building together at eight o'clock on conference evenings.) Just as Mary was about to flick off the classroom lights, two women walked into her classroom. They appeared annoyed and agitated. The older woman, a tall, thin individual in her early 30s, introduced herself as Jocelyn's aunt, Virginia Daniels. The younger woman was her daughter.

"What's this about Jocelyn getting grades of unsatisfactory and needs improvement on her report card?" the aunt asked in an antagonistic tone. "I demand to know why!" she continued, thrusting her fist in the air.

Mary was taken aback by her imperious manner and evident hostility; Virginia Daniels seemed on the verge of violence. She tried to stay calm herself and responded in an even tone, "I met with Jocelyn's grandmother earlier and explained why Jocelyn received the grades she did. I would be happy to meet with you to discuss Jocelyn's work another time, but teachers are required to leave the building at eight o'clock. Why don't you come tomorrow afternoon after school and we can talk then."

"I can't do that! I work. I can't get time off just for a meeting," Jocelyn's aunt said shrilly.

Mary was beginning to feel very apprehensive. "I'm sorry," she said, "it's just not possible for teachers to meet for conferences after eight o'clock."

Then Ms. Daniels's daughter turned to her mother. "She has to go out to her car," she noted quietly.

Now Mary really felt frightened. After all, she didn't know these two women; they just might be angry enough to harm her. "I really do need to leave now," she insisted, "so please call me to set up another appointment."

After the two women left, Mary quickly gathered her belongings and headed towards the principal's office. Mary described the incident to the principal, who promised to investigate it. Then, the staff walked out to the parking lot together.

When Mary got home, she made herself a hot cup of tea and thought about the day's events. She couldn't believe that after a full day of teaching and several conferences, she'd had an experience like that. She wondered if she should have handled it differently. She'd try to grab the principal and talk it over with her more the next day.

THE NEXT DAY

Soon after school ended the following day, Jocelyn's aunt arrived for a conference. Mary had just started to put up a new bulletin board. She was still jarred from her encounter with Ms. Daniels yesterday and piqued that she hadn't let her know she was coming. Still, she stopped everything to meet with her.

"You know I had to take a day off to come here," Jocelyn's aunt began in a huffy tone. "I'm sorry," said Mary, "but it's very important for us to talk about what's going on with Jocelyn." She explained the difficulties that Jocelyn was having, illustrating her comments with anecdotes and samples of Jocelyn's work. She reiterated the suggestions for home teaching that she had shared with Jocelyn's grandmother.

Jocelyn's aunt had calmed down and listened intently. Then she described, in a quiet voice, the tense situation with Jocelyn's mother. Moreover, she had been out of work for seven months and only last month landed a new job working in an office. Mary was sympathetic. Virginia Daniels might prove an ally in getting help for Jocelyn.

"You might want to talk with Mrs. Mark, the school social worker, for some suggestions," Mary advised. "I also think it would be a good idea to get Jocelyn tested. She has a hard time keeping up with the work the rest of the class is doing and spends long periods doing almost nothing. Then she disrupts the rest of the class."

"Absolutely not," Ms. Daniels replied, her hackles raised again. "I'll take care of helping her. I make her work for a long time on the computer every day, and I don't let her watch television at all. If there are problems, I'll take care of them." Ms. Daniels was beginning to seem more and more volatile to Mary. She wondered if Jocelyn would be punished.

"Perhaps we could both use a behavioral management chart with Jocelyn," Mary quickly suggested. She explained that this method tried to encourage appropriate behavior in a child by rewarding good behavior and denying privileges for misbehavior. On Fridays, Jocelyn would bring home her chart, and her aunt could add weekend tasks for her to complete. Mary would also send home extra assignments for Jocelyn to complete with her aunt's help. Ms. Daniels responded that these seemed like good ideas to her. As the conference ended, the two women agreed to keep in touch with each other.

Mary began to work on her bulletin board again. As she hung the children's paintings on the board, she reflected on the conference. Mary knew that Jocelyn's needs weren't being met right now in her classroom. She was pleased that Ms. Daniels and she had started to work together to help Jocelyn, and she felt that the behavior management plan was a good beginning. However, she wished she'd been able to convince Jocelyn's aunt that her niece should have a comprehensive evaluation. She wondered if the problems at home were the sole cause of Jocelyn's misbehavior at school and academic difficulties.

Discussion Questions

1. What problem(s) does Mary face?
2. What factors may have contributed to the problem(s)?
   - Consider factors at school.
   - Consider factors in Jocelyn's family.
3. How would you evaluate Mary's handling of the situation so far?
   - How would you analyze her recommendations to Jocelyn's grandmother? Please explain.
   - Comment on how Mary handled the situation when Jocelyn's aunt arrived at school at the end of the conference time. Should she have met with Ms. Daniels right then?
   - Should she have met with Jocelyn's aunt at all? Consider the legal issues.
4. What, if anything, should Mary do now?
   - Should she pursue the issue of testing Jocelyn and, if so, how?
   - Whom should Mary be communicating with—the grandmother or the aunt? How might she clarify the issue of who has custody of Jocelyn?
   - Are there other ways she might work with Jocelyn and her family? Please explain.
   - Whom in the school community might Mary call on to advise her and/or to help Jocelyn?

Suggested Activities

1. Role-play the conference between Mary and Virginia Daniels. Try to understand both characters' perspectives and represent them to each other. If you are role-playing Mary, suggest some new strategies that have not been mentioned in the case.
2. Review the literature on working with families under stress. Write a paper discussing the issues and recommended approaches.
3. Interview a school social worker. In his or her school, what guidelines should teachers follow in communicating with family members? What are the legal constraints when one family member has custody of the child?

Grounds for Divorce

CHARACTERS

Third-grade teacher:	Kate Bischoff
Student:	Jessie Bradford
Parents:	Rose and James Bradford
Grandmother:	Phyllis Bradford

Kate Bischoff, a third-grade teacher, hung up the phone and sighed. She had just spoken to the father of Jessie Bradford, a student in her class. Mr. Bradford had called to check whether Jessie's mom had dressed his daughter properly for the subzero weather. He quietly mentioned how lax Mrs. Bradford had become in caring for Jessie since their separation a year ago. Kate knew that they were in the process of a nasty divorce, and she had been receiving seemingly urgent complaints from both parents about each other since the year began. In fact, she had begun to feel like an operator for 911.

THE SCHOOL AND COMMUNITY

Jefferson Elementary School was located in East Lake, a city of 150,000. East Lake was a thriving cultural center, with a major art museum, a symphony orchestra, and several theaters. Its two universities provided stimulating lectures and inexpensive concerts to students and the larger community. Still, East Lake faced such problems as substandard housing, declining industry, and serious unemployment. Since the late 1980s, an increase in drug dealing and gang warfare had led to high levels of violent crime in many neighborhoods. In some of the poorer neighborhoods, parents tried to keep their children inside before and after school to avoid the random gunfire that often punctuated the air.

Jefferson's old brick school building housed a small kindergarten to fourth-grade program. The children were from varied socioeconomic and ethnic backgrounds. Several children were from faraway places like Germany and Thailand. They were often spending just a few years in the United States while their parents studied or worked at one of the city's universities. Proud of the diversity in the school, the teachers celebrated it in various ways. For example, parents and teachers organized an international fair each year, with refreshments and exhibits from the various countries represented in the student body.

Kate Bischoff had been teaching for eight years, and this was her second year at Jefferson. She particularly enjoyed teaching third grade. Her class consisted of 26 children, many from divorced or single-parent families. Kate thought it was important for the children to appreciate the differences among them. She also wanted them to feel free to talk about their concerns. She read stories about divorce and different family constellations so that the children would feel comfortable expressing their feelings and would realize that the topic was not taboo. She also listened to their parents, who often sought her advice.

In fact, since Jefferson emphasized the importance of family involvement in its program, Kate communicated frequently with family members. Parents volunteered in the classrooms, reading stories to children or carrying out special activities. They served on an advisory board to the school. At report card time, four times a year, parents were asked to meet personally with their children's teacher. Kate occasionally called parents to share "good news" about their children and they were comfortable calling her at home to make suggestions or discuss problems. She felt she had good rapport with most of the parents.

THE CHILD AND FAMILY

Jessie Bradford was eight years old. A large, lanky child, she was new to the school this year. She lived with her mother, Rose, and her younger brother. Because of her reduced income after the separation, Rose had moved to a poor neighborhood. She did not let her children play outside. The nearby park, with its broken glass and tough teenagers, represented the real dangers she saw lurking in the neighborhood for her children. Jessie had no friends in her new neighborhood.

Jessie's behavior had become increasingly distressing to Kate. Earlier in the year, she had thought that Jessie's withdrawn behavior might just be a sign of shyness and that she would open up as time went on. Now, in November, Jessie's moods seemed to swing between withdrawn and stridently aggressive.

At times, Jessie sat quietly, with a distant stare, not attending to her work. Often she gazed at the fish cruising about in the fish tank. At other times, she interacted comfortably with her classmates but then would suddenly turn on them and lash out. She might yell, shove, or yank another child's hair. Kate would separate Jessie and try to calm her, talking quietly about what had happened.

On these occasions, Jessie seemed remorseful and angry with herself. She realized that she was out of control but couldn't seem to stop herself. She tried to make up with her classmates, but they had grown aloof and self-protective after several such incidents. Sometimes she acted clownish as a way of getting their attention.

An intelligent child, Jessie had the ability to do well in school. She was articulate and enjoyed weaving elaborate stories during Writer's Workshop. She was intrigued by fantasies such as Roald Dahl's books. She also liked to draw. However, she often seemed tired and listless and complained about lack of sleep. She grumbled that her neighborhood was too noisy. Kate found that Jessie needed frequent attention and encouragement to complete her daily work.

Kate had spoken informally with Jessie's mother on a few occasions about Jessie's behavior. In her early 30s, Rose Bradford was struggling to piece her life back together. She was looking for a job and taking business courses at the local community college. During one of their talks, she confided to Kate. "I really need a job to support us all and haven't been able to find one. I'm so worried that I can't even concentrate on my schoolwork. It's so hard to juggle everything! And it burns me up that Jim has it so much easier—living in his mother's nice house and getting help from her. I'm afraid he'll take the kids from me." She was also worried that Jessie might run away from school, as she had last year.

James Bradford was a manager in a local supermarket. After the separation, he had sold his modest but comfortable suburban house and moved to his mother's home in the same town. Jessie and her brother spent weekends with their father and grandmother. Her dad was an avid gardener, and helped Jessie work a plot of her own. She and her dad also enjoyed cooking together, especially their home-grown vegetables. On Mondays, Jessie chattered vivaciously about the fun she'd had over the weekend, riding her bike and visiting her old friends. As the week went on, she tended to grow more silent.

Rose and Jim had agreed that Rose would have custody of the children while the divorce was pending. However, now Jim was fighting to gain permanent custody of the children as part of the final order. He felt the children were living in unsafe circumstances and that Rose was unfit as a mother. Although he worked long hours, he frequently called Kate to discuss his worries. He said he planned to come in for an evening conference soon.

Kate listened to Jim but tried to maintain her focus on Jessie. "I know that you're all struggling through a difficult time," she said, "but let's think about how we can help Jessie right now". But Jim seemed unable to hear her concerns or to work with her to develop solutions. He continually blamed his wife and couldn't move beyond that. The custody battle had grown very bitter. In fact, Jim and Rose had each asked Kate to testify on their behalf.

Jim's mother, Phyllis, was a warm, cheery woman in her late 50s. She adored her grandchildren and occasionally came to school to read a story to their classes or to have lunch with them. When the children were sick, she picked them up from school. She told Kate she believed that Rose verbally abused the children. She was convinced that they would be better off living away from their mother in a safer neighborhood with their father and her.

Kate cautioned Phyllis not to speak negatively about Rose in front of her children. She talked with Phyllis about Jessie's behavior at school. Phyllis had seen Jessie's violent outbursts directed at her little brother at home and she was concerned. Kate and Phyllis shared the goal of convincing Jessie's parents that their daughter's problems must be identified and dealt with.

However, whenever Kate tried to discuss Jessie's difficulties with Rose, Rose seemed distracted and diverted the conversation to her own problems. Her own family was in the city, but they didn't seem available for emotional or financial support. Rose ridiculed her husband and his mother and accused them of turning the children against her. Rose even implied that her mother-in-law was pushing her son to fight with her in order to punish her. Although Rose cared about her children, she seemed unable to follow even Kate's simplest suggestions about ways to help Jessie, such as establishing a regular bedtime routine.

NEXT STEPS?

Kate was at her wit's end. She felt caught in a vise between two warring parents, and a grandmother to boot! She didn't want Jessie to get lost in the fray. She wondered if Jessie, too, had been exposed to the constant crossfire and criticism between the important people in her life.

Typically, Kate liked to have both parents come to the conference, even in a divorce situation. But this was far from an amicable separation and she didn't want the whole thing to blow up in her face.

Discussion Questions

1. What problem(s) is Kate facing?
2. How did this situation develop? Identify the underlying issues in this case.
   - What might be the causes of Jessie's behavior?
   - How might each of the family members be contributing to her difficulties?
   - Could Kate be contributing to the problems? If so, how?
3. How do you think the problem(s) is (are) perceived from the vantages of Kate, Rose, Jim, and Jessie?
4. What further information would you like in order to make a decision?
5. If you were the teacher, what would you do at this point to resolve the problem(s)?
   - Would you invite both parents to the conference or would you speak to them individually? Should the grandmother be invited? Why?
   - What would you say at the conference to help Jessie's parents understand her behavior?
   - Should Kate testify in court on behalf of either parent?

- How would you get the parents' help in proposing and carrying out strategies to help Jessie?
- What strategies might you suggest?
6. What other school personnel might Kate call upon to help her?

Suggested Activities

1. Imagine that you are the teacher in this case. Explain the situation to a support person in your school, such as the principal or school psychologist, who might be able to provide some guidance to you.
2. Role-play the possible parent-teacher conference(s) between Kate and Jessie's family members.
3. Write a research paper on the effects of divorce on young children. Identify ways that schools can help children and parents cope with divorce.

The Bully

It was a crisp January day and the sun shone brightly—a sign of warmer weather to come. Jim Slavin's fifth graders were outside for recess. Scattered across the large yard, the children were engaged in a variety of activities from jump rope to an informal soccer game. While supervising the soccer game, Jim suddenly heard shouts from a far corner. He rushed over to the crowd of children that had formed and broke through their circle. At the center of the circle, George Silensky, a hefty 10-year-old, was straddling Arthur Anderson and pummeling him relentlessly. George's two friends, Ryan and Lonnie, were cheering him on. Jim quickly separated the entangled boys and dispersed the crowd. His mind raced as he thought about what to do next to handle this situation.

THE SCHOOL AND COMMUNITY

Lawrence was a town of about 30,000 in the Pequot River valley. Most factories had closed in this once-thriving mill town, and few new industries had replaced them. People scraped together a living as best they could, primarily working in the small businesses and service industries that had held on in the faltering economy.

West Side Elementary School was a large, two-story brick structure built in the 1930s. Despite recent renovations, the building had plumbing problems, and even a fresh coat of paint couldn't relieve its pervasive dreariness.

Moreover, as the tax base in the community had eroded, fewer funds were being allocated for education.

There were over 500 students in the kindergarten through fifth grades. Classes were packed, with 28 to 30 students in each, and resources were sparse. There was one full-time special education teacher. The school psychologist and social worker had heavy case loads and divided their time between two schools. There were long periods when the school had no psychological support system.

Jim Slavin had been teaching for two years. He had grown up in a nearby town and had attended the local state university while working part-time to finance his education. He majored in history and got certified in teaching. With his small, sturdy frame, he became a valued member of the college's wrestling team.

The oldest child in a family of four children, he frequently helped out with the care of his siblings. He had always been involved with kids in one way or another. He had been a Big Brother in high school and held camp counseling jobs for several summers. It seemed natural for him to go into teaching. Jim was delighted when he landed this job at West Side. The first year had been a shock—he hadn't realized that teaching would be so complicated. He found himself spending hours writing lesson plans, collecting materials, and thinking about how to handle problems that arose in the class. However, he loved the interaction with his students and was pleased with his small successes. This second year had been easier for him, and he was enjoying his job even more. George had been his major hurdle.

GEORGE AND HIS FAMILY

George Silensky was a strong, hefty boy, proud of his physical prowess, who seemed to swagger. He had been taking karate since he was seven.

George was the youngest of five children. Harry Silensky, his father, was an auto mechanic in a local garage. The family was strapped financially, and George's parents frequently fought over money. In September, when the children went back to school, Susan Silensky got a part-time job at a local fast food restaurant to help make ends meet. She worked from 5:00 to 10:00 P.M. During the day, she spent her time cleaning the house so it would meet with her husband's high standards.

The children were often left to their own resources. The older brothers and sisters had always had major responsibility for taking care of George, who particularly admired his brother Steve. A teenager, Steve frequently butted heads with Mr. Silensky over curfews and the use of the car. Although his father would rant and rave, if Steve insisted Mr. Silensky caved in and handed over the keys. Mrs. Silensky worried about car accidents, but she stood by helplessly during their arguments. Mr. Silensky told her to shut up if she tried to intervene.

Mr. Silensky took care of the children in the evenings. "Every night, my dad drinks his beer and watches TV," George said to his teacher one day. George was rarely in bed before 11:00 at night and was often tired in the mornings.

George's grades were average. He especially enjoyed math and liked to compete in the computation contests that Jim held periodically. Once, as a captain, he led his team to victory. He mercilessly teased the students on the losing team and when Jim intervened, he responded with a smirk. He stopped for a while but when Jim glanced at him later, he was taunting some children again. Jim rebuked him, but George denied that he was doing anything wrong.

Despite his domineering behavior, George enjoyed a certain popularity. His cocky attitude had made him a particular favorite of two other boys, Ryan and Lonnie. The three friends palled around together. They rode the same bus home and often played after school. Arthur rode that bus as well.

ARTHUR AND HIS FAMILY

Sheila Anderson gave birth to Arthur when she was 18. Arthur's father, whom she did not marry, soon left town and was not involved in his upbringing. Ms. Anderson once had vague plans of attending the community college but she needed to work to support her young child. She went to a local hairdressing academy and now worked in a downtown beauty parlor. Her parents, who lived in Lawrence, had tried to help her care for Arthur when he was younger. In recent years, her father had become chronically ill, and her mother was busy with his care.

Arthur and his mother lived in a modest two-bedroom apartment. Elderly citizens rented the other apartments in the building. Although Arthur had no friends in the neighborhood, he enjoyed visiting his neighbors. One woman had taken a grandmotherly interest in him and often offered him milk and cookies after school. When his mother came home from work, she'd kick off her shoes, and they would watch television together for a while. After dinner, she helped him with his homework.

Arthur was both small and young for his class. To avoid additional day-care costs, his mother had enrolled him in kindergarten as a four-and-a-half-year-old. Many of the other fifth-grade boys now loomed over him.

Jim observed that Arthur rarely raised his hand in class or volunteered for an activity. When called upon, he responded tentatively. It was hard to hear his whisper. He often double-checked his work with Jim, to make sure that he was doing it correctly. He performed at an average level and didn't seem to have any special strengths or interests. Recently, he had been absent more. Because Arthur seemed so frail, Jim wasn't surprised.

On the playground, Arthur was cautious. From a safe distance, he watched the other boys in their rough-and-tumble play. Jim seldom saw him interacting with others. He was generally one of the last children chosen for teams in organized games. Recently, Jim had begun to pair Arthur with other children for projects, with the goal of sparking a friendship. The other children complied but didn't seem eager to work with Arthur.

TELEPHONE CALLS TO THE HOMES

After the brawl on the playground, Jim spoke to both Arthur and George firmly to let them know how unhappy he was with their behavior. With a downcast expression, Arthur simply stood and listened. George claimed that Arthur had been taunting him by calling him "Georgy Porgy" and had refused to stop.

Although this story seemed unlikely to Jim, he hadn't witnessed the precipitating events. He told the boys that he would need to report the incident to their parents. Then he would determine appropriate punishments.

Right after school he telephoned Ms. Anderson first because he had already met her. She had seemed timid, like her son. At the first parent-teacher conference, in November, she expressed quiet appreciation for Jim's work and genuine interest in Arthur's progress. She also openly described her struggles as a teen parent.

Now, after hearing about the playground fight, Ms. Anderson poured forth a story. "I've been very worried about Arthur, but he begged me not to tell you," she confessed. "Arthur says George has been bullying him since December."

One day, in the boys' bathroom, George had stuffed Arthur's book bag into the toilet. Another day, Arthur had come home late from school. Apparently, George, Lonnie, and Ryan had blocked him in his seat on the bus and had refused to let him get off at his stop. Arthur had been afraid to protest, and the bus driver, unaware, had continued on his way. After George and his friends got off, Arthur approached the bus driver and explained the situation. At the end of the route, the driver took Arthur home. George and his friends had also threatened to beat up Arthur if he didn't bring them candy or gum. Ms. Anderson now understood why Arthur's allowance had disappeared so quickly.

Recently, Arthur had been complaining about headaches in the morning; he wanted to stay home from school. Two days earlier, when his mother had questioned him, he described what was happening with George. He insisted that his mother keep it a secret, however, because George warned that he would break his arm if he told. Arthur was utterly terrified.

Ms. Anderson had been unsure how to handle this. Just this morning, she had resolved to call the school, and she was actually relieved when Jim's call came. Ms. Anderson's account of Arthur's experiences sent chills up Jim's spine. He realized that George was aggressive and impulsive, but he never thought that he was capable of such hostile behavior.

The call to George's parents would be even more difficult than Jim had expected. Since they had not come to the November conference, he had no personal contact with them. However, he had some knowledge of the family situation from George's casual comments in class and his journal entries.

When his mother had gone to work, George had mentioned the family tension in his journal.

The phone rang several times before Mr. Silensky picked it up. Jim introduced himself as George's teacher and then described the incident on the playground. He planned to invite Mr. and Mrs. Silensky to school for a conference, but before he could suggest it, Mr. Silensky reacted strongly to the story. "I don't know why you're all upset over a playground fight. Those kinds of things used to happen all the time when I was in school. It's just boys having fun. Besides, they need to learn to protect themselves. That's why I sent George to learn karate."

Jim was dumbfounded. He hadn't expected the father to dismiss his son's actions in such a cavalier way. But he felt George's total pattern of behavior, as described by Ms. Anderson, was too important to discuss over the telephone.

How should he handle the phone conversation with Mr. Silensky right now? How could he enlist the help of the parents in dealing with their sons' behaviors? What role should he take to stop George's bullying and to help Arthur to learn to assert himself?

Discussion Questions

1. What problem(s) does Jim face?
2. How did this situation develop?
3. How might George's family situation contribute to his behavior?
   - Who are his role models?
   - How might the child-rearing style of his parents have affected him?
4. What factors might contribute to Arthur's behavior?
   - Who are his role models?
   - How might the child-rearing style of his mother have affected him?
5. Does Arthur's behavior make him a likely victim? Why or why not?
6. How should Jim respond to Mr. Silensky's comments over the phone?
7. How can he gain the support of the parents in dealing with their sons' behaviors?
8. Should he bring all of the parents together for a conference? Why or why not?
9. What, if any, is Jim's role in modifying George's and Arthur's behavior?

Suggested Activities

1. Role-play the telephone call between Jim and Mr. Silensky. Try out various ways that Jim might respond to Mr. Silensky.
2. Role-play the following conferences:
   - between Jim and Mr. and Mrs. Silensky
   - between Jim and Ms. Anderson
   - between Jim and both sets of parents

Consider whether other professionals should be involved, and if so, which ones and for what purpose?

3. Interview a special education teacher who has worked with students with behavior disorders. What strategies has she or he found effective to help the student in the classroom? What recommendations has she or he made to parents?

4. Write a research paper on the problem of bullying. What factors contribute to the problem? What school interventions have been successful?

New Kid on the Block

CHARACTERS

Kindergarten teacher:	Beth Arman
Student:	Dan Goodman
Parent:	Mrs. Goodman

Beth Arman, a teacher, was leading her kindergarten's daily meeting time. It was Tuesday, and Dan's mother, Mrs. Goodman, was volunteering as usual in the class. She sat at the edge of the circle and seemed to survey the scene coldly. Beth sensed Mrs. Goodman's disapproval but tried to ignore it. Then Jeffrey called out an answer to her question, and Beth harshly rebuked the young child for not raising his hand. His face contorted and tears welled in his eyes.

"Oh, oh," thought Beth, "this is really getting to me."

THE SCHOOL AND COMMUNITY

Clearview was an elementary school for children in kindergarten through fifth grades in the suburb of Lathrop. The community was middle class, and many parents worked in the pharmaceutical industry in the town. They tried to offer their children every advantage. It was not uncommon for the elementary school children to have a full schedule of sports, music and art lessons, or scout meetings after school.

Built in the early 1970s, the school was originally designed for an "open classroom" approach to education, with large rooms for teachers to team-teach two classes. After abandoning the open classroom philosophy years ago, the school had tried to adapt the building to a more traditional layout. Now, portable room dividers offered a visual barrier between classes, but sound still carried across the dividers.

Clearview had a new principal who prided himself on keeping up with educational innovations particularly family involvement. He had read the studies that indicated that greater family involvement in schools was associated with higher student achievement. While Clearview's parents had always shown a strong interest in their children's education, the principal was urging teachers to involve the parents on a regular basis in the classrooms.

Beth Arman was also new to Clearview. She had graduated from the local state university two years earlier. A conscientious and successful student, she was pleased to land a job as a fourth-grade teacher at Clearview. Although her first year had the normal difficulties, by June she felt that she was finally adjusting to the rigorous demands of teaching. After this year's introduction to fourth grade, she looked forward to refining the curriculum and her skills in the same grade the next year.

Unfortunately, at the very end of the year, the kindergarten teacher announced her retirement, and the principal asked Beth to take over the kindergarten in the fall. The thought of making the transition from fourth graders to very young children made Beth apprehensive. However, as a new teacher, she didn't feel she was in a position to question his decision.

Beth started the new year with trepidation, but she tried to meet her principal's expectations. In early September, she sent home a letter encouraging parents to participate in the classroom and an accompanying questionnaire asking them to identify interests they might share with the children. She suggested, for example, that parents might talk to the class about their work, chaperone trips, or share aspects of their cultural traditions. She was pleased to receive positive responses from several parents.

THE STUDENT AND THE FAMILY

One mother, Mrs. Goodman, offered to come regularly once a week to conduct an activity, such as cooking or art, with the children. She was a former teacher herself who was taking time off from her career to care for her two young children. In fact, she had taught previously at this very school. Her husband was a biologist. Dan was her first child.

Dan Goodman started kindergarten in September as a four-and-a-half-year-old. Because of his age, his parents had considered delaying the start of school another year for him. However, he had enjoyed his two years of nursery school, seemed comfortable in group situations, and was verbally advanced, so they chose to send him to kindergarten.

Having taught kindergarten herself, Mrs. Goodman felt that Dan was ready and would enjoy the varied kindergarten experiences. She talked with him about the different centers he'd see in the classroom, such as the block area, dress ups, reading corner, and math area. He seemed excited about going to school. On the first day of school, the whole family walked the bouncy, tow-headed child to school.

TENSIONS DEVELOP

Although Beth liked the idea of some family involvement, she was not sure that she wanted a parent in her classroom on a regular basis. The thought of sharing her class with someone who was both a mother and an experienced teacher made her particularly apprehensive. However, she didn't feel she could say no to Mrs. Goodman's offer.

On her first visit, Mrs. Goodman made applesauce with the children. She was dynamic and well organized, and the children were intrigued by the activity. When Beth saw how the children benefited, she, too, was pleased. She even felt that she might learn from Mrs. Goodman's example.

However, as time went on, Beth began to dread Mrs. Goodman's Tuesday visits. When Mrs. Goodman arrived, she appeared to scrutinize the room haughtily. She made asides about the lack of children's artwork on the walls or commented that it might be nice to teach them a few new finger plays. When she suggested that Beth might want to send a monthly newsletter home to parents to describe classroom experiences, Beth gulped at the thought of more work. She felt she was being judged and was overloaded as it was!

Beth also had a gnawing feeling that the children preferred Mrs. Goodman to her. Every Tuesday morning, when Dan's mother arrived, the children rushed to her and hugged her warmly. They looked forward to the appealing activities she shared with them. Once she brought in a turtle; another time, the children made patterns with natural objects, such as bright red maple leaves, acorns, and feathery ferns. Although Dan had clung to his mother during her first two visits, he now seemed comfortable sharing her with the other children.

In fact, Beth felt that Dan was doing fine in general, but Mrs. Goodman would occasionally question her practices with him. One time, she asked why Dan had been allowed to work in the block area all week during center time. She knew that he wasn't rotating through the learning centers because in the evenings he eagerly described the buildings that he had constructed every day. Beth explained to Mrs. Goodman that this occurred during the one week when the kindergarten teachers traditionally assessed the children individually for skill development. During that week, as the teachers worked with individual children, the others were allowed to choose any center they wished. Still, the mother seemed concerned. Beth was beginning to feel that she couldn't do anything right.

MRS. GOODMAN'S PERSPECTIVE

By mid-October, Mrs. Goodman had expected Dan to know several songs and to recite some simple poetry. She had expected progress sheets telling parents how they could help their children at home. She had looked for paintings or art projects to display proudly on the refrigerator. But not much was coming home. When she spoke with the parents of other kindergartners in the class, they, too, had seen little evidence of their children's work.

The few times that Dan had brought home papers, they were incomplete and their purpose wasn't clear. Mrs. Goodman didn't know whether or not she was supposed to help him to finish the work.

On her weekly visits, she continued to be disappointed by the lack of "life" in the room. She saw the classroom as plain and uninviting. She had subtly suggested ways to decorate the room to Beth, but Beth didn't follow up on them.

She was also disturbed because she felt that the children frequently misbehaved. Beth didn't seem to have established clear rules and guidelines, and she responded inconsistently to the children. One day, Mrs. Goodman observed Jeffrey, a particularly difficult child, hitting Dan. Beth was working with another child and didn't even seem to notice. Mrs. Goodman tried to alert Beth to the problem, but Beth didn't intervene. Finally, Mrs. Goodman went to help her son. Later, Mrs. Goodman attempted to raise the possibility with Beth that Jeffrey might have special needs. Moreover, Mrs. Goodman thought that Jeffrey was taking too much of Beth's attention, and the other 22 children in the class were being neglected. Although Beth listened to her politely, she didn't really appear to want to discuss the problem.

Mrs. Goodman was very disappointed and concerned for Dan. She had attempted to give Beth as much concrete assistance in the classroom as possible. When she had tried delicately to discuss some of her concerns with Beth, Beth had been defensive.

Mrs. Goodman commented, "We wanted Dan to have a wonderful kindergarten experience, with an intuitive, dynamic teacher. I feel cheated, as a parent, that he did not get the very best in this teacher. I have been trying to make mental notes to remind myself of what it is like to sit on both sides of the desk. It's not easy to be a struggling teacher, trying to make the best of a difficult situation. But it's not easy for a parent to place her child in someone else's hands, either."

THE LAST STRAW

The relationship between Beth and Mrs. Goodman became more and more strained. On Tuesdays, Beth felt that her classroom was no longer her own.

One Wednesday, in late November, she was eating lunch with another teacher, Liz, in the teacher's lounge. They were the only teachers in the room, and she began to confide her concerns to Liz. After listening sympathetically to Beth, Liz hesitated. Then Liz revealed she had heard that Mrs. Goodman had told another teacher on the staff, a friend, that she was disappointed with Beth's teaching. The rumor mill was churning.

Discussion Questions

1. What problem(s) is Beth facing?
2. What underlying issues do you see in this case?
3. How did this situation develop?
4. How might it have been avoided?
5. Evaluate Mrs. Goodman's perspective.
   - How valid is it?
   - Is she expecting too much of a new teacher?
   - What else might she have done?
6. Evaluate Beth's perspective.
   - How valid is it?
   - Should Beth have limited Mrs. Goodman's involvement in order to protect herself as a new teacher?
   - Is this a management issue or a personality issue?
7. If you were Beth, what would you do to resolve the problem(s)?
   - Would you meet with Mrs. Goodman to discuss the problem? If so, what would you say?
   - Would you involve other school personnel? If so, whom and how? Is there a role for a mentor teacher in this situation?
8. What lessons might Beth draw from this experience for her future work with parents? As she becomes more experienced, is this problem likely to recur?

Suggested Activities

1. Role-play a meeting in late November to try to solve the situation. Identify who will be at the meeting. Alternate the roles of the various participants, so that you develop an understanding of each point of view.
2. Develop a sheet of guidelines for parents for working in a classroom.
3. Develop a questionnaire to identify parents' interests and skills that might be shared in the classroom.
4. Visit a school that tries to foster family involvement. Interview the administrators and teachers to identify ways that the school has successfully involved family members. Discuss problems that have developed and ask how the school has handled these.

Whose Problem Is It?

CHARACTERS

First-grade teacher:	Jean Merman
Teacher's aide:	Diane Jones
Principal:	Emily Vincent
Student:	Sean Kennedy
Parents:	Muriel and Joseph Kennedy

Jean Merman, a first-grade teacher, sighed as she put down the phone. Sean Kennedy, her student, had reported to his mother that the school nurse had checked the children for head lice. Now Mrs. Kennedy was calling to find out if the teachers' aides were also being checked as possible transmitters of the lice. If Mrs. Kennedy was so concerned, Jean wondered, why was she targeting the aides and not asking about the teachers as well?

THE SCHOOL, COMMUNITY, AND TEACHER

Roosevelt Elementary School was a magnet school in Portland, a city of 125,000. It had a special emphasis on math and science education, and the children's standardized test scores were routinely among the highest in the city. Parents vied to have their children accepted into the program. Enrollment was based on a lottery system, and children from varied racial, ethnic, and socioeconomic groups throughout the city were represented.

Teachers in the school were generally highly committed and enthusiastic. Moreover, there were full-time aides in the lower grades because the school had received additional monies through grants. Many of the aides were parents whose children had attended the program, and most were members of minority groups. Although they had not received formal teacher training, they were carefully screened by the staff for their ability to work with children.

Jean Merman had been teaching at Roosevelt for seven years. She had done her student teaching in the program and had been pleased with the developmental approach of the school and the professional attitude of the staff. She was delighted to be offered a position there.

For the last two years, Diane Jones had been Jean's aide. Diane's son was in high school now but had attended elementary school at Roosevelt. Diane was tall and energetic. Although she was sometimes a little gruff with the children, Jean felt that Diane's heart was in the right place. Moreover, Diane was an open and growing person who happily attended the school's in-service training workshops and continued to develop new teaching skills.

THE CHILD AND FAMILY

Sean Kennedy came from a family of six children. His father was a policeman and his mother worked in a supermarket. Both parents wanted their children to get good educations and move into professional fields as adults. Joseph Kennedy frequently expressed the desire that all his children go to college. The Kennedys chose Roosevelt School because it was considered outstanding among Portland's programs.

Sean was a wiry six-year-old. He loved to construct things and was adept at creating interesting vehicles and buildings with Legos. He also enjoyed natural science and knew an enormous amount about wild animals and dinosaurs. A shy child, he was just beginning to feel comfortable expressing himself at circle time by November. While other children occasionally tested the rules, he scrupulously obeyed them and seemed fearful of doing anything wrong.

The school tried to promote positive parent-teacher relationships, and occasionally the kindergarten and first-grade teachers made home visits, if parents were agreeable. The teachers had found that sometimes parents were more relaxed and comfortable on their own "turf" with teachers. This was an opportunity for the teachers to develop a special rapport with both the parents and the child.

Because of Sean's shyness, Jean had felt that a home visit might be useful. In mid-September, she called Mrs. Kennedy to make a date, and Mrs. Kennedy seemed pleased.

During the visit, Mrs. Kennedy expressly asked about the training that the aides received. She explained that Sean had had a negative experience with a soccer coach who was just learning the ropes. (In an aside, she mentioned that the coach was black. The Kennedys lived in an all-white neighborhood, though the city had a high percentage of minorities.) Jean reassured Mrs. Kennedy that the aides received regular in-service training at the school and that they were closely supervised by the classroom teachers.

THE PROBLEMS DEVELOP

Mrs. Kennedy occasionally came to Sean's class to help out. On a mid-October day when she was there, Diane was supervising a group of children who were carrying out a math activity with the Unifix cubes. When clean-up time was announced, one child, David, rushed away from the table to get in line for the bathroom. Diane set aside a small collection of cubes for David to put away and asked the other children to put the rest in the container. Then, she went over to David and asked him to return to the table to clean up. When he refused, Diane firmly took his hand and led him there. At that point, he started to put the remaining cubes away.

Apparently, Mrs. Kennedy had watched this scene from the other side of the room. Later Jean learned from her principal, Emily Vincent, that Mrs. Kennedy had complained that Diane had handled the child very roughly. Since Jean had not directly observed the incident, she felt that she could not comment on Diane's actions to Mrs. Vincent. However, she hadn't received any complaints from David or his parents.

Jean was annoyed that Mrs. Kennedy had not spoken to her first about the issue, rather than going to the principal, yet she wanted to give the mother the benefit of the doubt. Maybe Mrs. Kennedy had run into the principal in the hall and just blurted out her concern.

But, two weeks later, Jean was really taken aback when Mrs. Kennedy lodged another complaint against Diane, relating the following upsetting experience her son had had.

On Friday, Jean was at a meeting, and Diane covered the class for an hour. The children were at their tables doing some worksheets. They occasionally conferred with each other, as was customary when a child needed help.

The children at Sean's table were usually focused and applied themselves to work. However, there had been no recess the past few days because of rain, and they were excited about finally going outdoors later on this sunny day. They became fidgety and their talk grew louder and louder. First Diane asked them to be quieter. When they didn't keep their voices low, she told them that they could not talk at all.

Then one boy's loud voice punctuated the air. Losing patience, Diane shouted, "I told you to shut up! Now, none of you at that table will have recess, and you're in for a real punishment on Monday when Mrs. Vincent finds out!"

When Sean came home from school that day, Mrs. Kennedy hurried her children into the car to go to a doctor's appointment. It wasn't until bedtime, when she was kissing Sean goodnight, that he burst into tears and told her about this experience. He seemed panicked about the unknown punishment that lay in wait for him on Monday—the possibility of having to go to the principal's office terrified him.

At the same time, he was angry. A logical child, he didn't think it was fair that all of the children were being punished for one child's mistake. He also felt that the loss of recess was sufficient punishment.

Unfortunately, Mrs. Kennedy didn't hear this story until eight o'clock on Friday night, so she couldn't call school to ask Jean to reassure her son. At bedtime on both Saturday and Sunday nights, the six-year-old again dissolved in tears and was inconsolable.

On Monday morning, Mrs. Kennedy took Sean to school and asked to speak with Jean. By this time, the mother was really angry. She expressed outrage that a young child could have been frightened so badly by an adult. She wanted the school to reevaluate whether Diane had the necessary skills for her position.

As Jean listened to Mrs. Kennedy's story, she felt genuine concern at the description of Diane's handling of the situation. But, she also had an underlying worry that there might be more to this than just teaching skills. She had begun to suspect that Mrs. Kennedy might be prejudiced against Diane because she was African-American. Now, what should she do?

Discussion Questions

1. What dilemma(s) does Jean face? What underlying issues are there?
2. Could this situation have been avoided? If so, how?
    • Could Jean have foreseen that this problem was coming? Should she have nipped it in the bud, and, if so, how?
    • Should parents be formally advised of the role of the aides in the school?
    • Should aides have more training? If so, what kind of training would you recommend?
3. Evaluate the strength of Mrs. Kennedy's complaints about Diane.
4. Evaluate the strength of Jean's concern that Mrs. Kennedy may be prejudiced.
5. How should Jean deal with the situation at this point?
    • Should Jean handle this herself? Should she ask for help from someone else in the school and, if so, whom? What are the advantages and disadvantages of each?
    • Develop a strategy for Jean to solve this dilemma.

Suggested Activities

1. Role-play the meeting between Jean and Muriel Kennedy at which Mrs. Kennedy complains about Diane and asks for the school to evaluate her.
2. Interview two teachers who have aides working in their classrooms. What are the pros and cons of working with aides? Have there been any parent complaints about the aides? If so, what were the complaints and how did the teachers handle the situations?
3. Interview administrators at two schools where aides work in the classrooms. What strategies, if any, does the school use to prepare the aide for working in the classroom? Are parents informed in a systematic way of the role of the aides in the classroom and, if so, how?

4. Whether or not you conclude that prejudice was involved in this particular case, investigate ways that schools can address the issue of prejudice among students, teachers, and parents. Write a paper describing these strategies.

What More Can I Do?

CHARACTERS

| First-grade teachers: | Theresa Ayala |
| | Marie Santos |

Theresa Ayala anxiously watched the clock, hoping that at least a few more parents would show up for her first grade's Thanksgiving show. The children had worked for weeks to practice songs, make costumes, and create sets. Moreover, she and Marie, the school's other bilingual teacher, had prepared a delicious Thanksgiving supper of roast turkey, stuffing, cranberry sauce, Spanish rice, bread and butter, drinks, and cake for dessert.

The show had been scheduled for a lunch hour the week before Thanksgiving, so it wouldn't feel like an extra demand on families during the busy holiday week. The children in both bilingual classes had personally designed and sent invitations to their parents and had asked the parents to R.S.V.P. Of the 36 parents, only seven responded to say they would come.

It was 11:55 A.M. now. The show was scheduled to begin in five minutes, but only one parent had arrived. Theresa sighed as she looked around at the walls decorated with the children's artwork depicting the first Thanksgiving. The tables sported child-decorated tablecloths and pinecone turkey centerpieces.

By 12:05, four more parents had arrived, and Theresa nodded to Marie to begin the children's singing. At that point, one child, Carmen, tugged at her sleeve. "Wait, wait!" she insisted, "I know my mother's coming! She told me she would." Theresa reassured Carmen and held up the show for a few minutes, but Carmen's mother never arrived.

THE SCHOOL AND COMMUNITY

East Side Elementary School was located in Chesterton, a city of about 100,000. Hispanics were the largest and fastest-growing population, and there was also a substantial African-American community. Whites were a minority. Chesterton was an old factory town whose industries had not kept up with technological advances and had closed due to declining business. There were high rates of unemployment, poverty, and drug abuse. It was not uncommon for elementary schoolchildren to witness a shooting or stabbing. Guns had been confiscated in the area high schools.

East Side School had about 400 students, 90 percent from Hispanic families. Most parents were not working, and most families depended upon public assistance. Eighty percent of the children in the school qualified for free lunches.

East Side's strong bilingual program was a transitional model, which meant in the morning, non-English-speaking children received instruction in Spanish in all curriculum areas, and in the afternoon they were taught the English language. This allowed their learning to continue in areas such as social studies, reading, and math while they also acquired English. Then, as their English skills advanced, they were taught increasingly more of the basic curriculum in their new language.

THE TEACHER AND HER CLASS

Theresa Ayala, an intense, dynamic woman, had moved to this country from Puerto Rico at the age of two. She came from a poor family and was the oldest of five children. She had always been involved with youngsters; for many years, she worked as a counselor in her town's summer programs.

During her school years, several teachers recognized Theresa's ability and encouraged her. She worked hard, did well, and obtained a scholarship to a prestigious university in the state.

She majored in political science and planned to go on to law school after college. Shortly after she graduated, a friend persuaded Theresa to become a teacher. Because of the need for bilingual teachers, Theresa was given an emergency certificate. She now had been teaching for seven years and had become certified. She felt a strong commitment to teaching—and never regretted her decision. "I've never looked back," she told a friend.

Theresa had 18 children in her class, all of whom had been identified as needing remedial help. When the year began, some children could not count past the number five or recognize the first five numerals. There was one child who had suffered from fetal alcohol syndrome as a baby and another who had been born to a mother with AIDS. Although that child did not have AIDS, she did have learning problems. During the course of the year, four of Theresa's students would be formally identified as having special needs and two others were likely to be identified in the near future.

The children also had many strengths. They wanted to learn and eagerly participated in the many experiential activities that Theresa provided. "Of course they squabble, but for the most part they're caring kids. They always have hugs for each other and me," she explained.

Theresa had an assistant four days a week, and together they worked to individualize the instruction as much as possible. The assistant taught the three higher-level reading groups, and Theresa took responsibility for the two lower groups. One child was reading in English. By spring, some children were at the level of combining word puzzles to make sentences, while others were reading books at their grade level. All of the children had made some improvement.

Emphasis was placed on the basic subject areas, but Theresa acknowledged the developmental need of young children to have hands-on instruction and this fidgety group's particular need to have plenty of opportunity to move. For example, she enjoyed promoting language and concept development through role playing.

She also used a variety of motivational strategies, including small toys or a pizza party as rewards for good effort. "I spend my money as if these were my own children," she once commented. In addition to their regular instruction from Theresa and her assistant, the children had art, music, and gym as specials and used a computerized writing program.

INVOLVING THE PARENTS

Theresa worked energetically to involve the parents in their children's education. She helped write a monthly newsletter, in both Spanish and English, which described upcoming schoolwide events and special activities in the classrooms.

After the Thanksgiving show, Theresa and Marie invited the parents and the school community to a Christmas show. The show was held at 10:00 A.M. on a Tuesday morning—the only time that the gym was available. Each teacher contributed $150.00 for materials, and the assistants worked for weeks making colorful traditional Puerto Rican costumes for the children to wear.

At the show, the girls were dressed in long skirts, white shirts, and sashes. The boys wore pants, shirts, sashes and scarves. The children sang both American and Spanish Christmas songs and recited poetry in both languages. They danced and played traditional Puerto Rican instruments, including tambourines, maracas, and the guiro. However, the turnout was very disappointing; out of both classes, only one parent came to the show.

In May, Theresa and her children decided to produce a play in English for the entire school community and the parents. The children practiced for a month, because Theresa wanted to be sure that they really understood what they were saying. In addition, they worked industriously to make the sets, eagerly coloring, gluing, and pasting in anticipation of the big event. Still, only one parent attended the play. The children scoffed down the cake and juice planned for the reception, but the coffee went untouched.

Theresa felt frustrated that she had not been able to involve the families more in their children's education. "It's not only these special events that parents miss. They don't even come to school for report card conferences," she commented.

However, there was at least one area of partial success. Each child had a spiral notebook, and every day Theresa conscientiously wrote a message to every child's parent, in Spanish. Each evening, parents were asked to help the children with their spelling words. In addition, there were concrete suggestions of how to help in areas of individual need. For example, if a child was having difficulty adding, Theresa would suggest to the parent a strategy for helping her.

Seventy-five percent of the parents wrote back to Theresa. One might comment, "Thank you. That was a good idea. It helped." Another might respond, "This kid seems to understand one minute and not the next." If a child reported to Theresa that his parents hadn't worked with him, Theresa might write, "Your child says that you haven't helped him all week." Sometimes the parent responded, "That's not true. I sat with him but he didn't want to work."

WHAT MORE CAN I DO?

Theresa was disappointed with the parents. Although some parents worked hard with their children and the children showed improvement, Theresa felt that 25 percent of the children wouldn't be able to succeed in second grade. She was frustrated that these children were not at the level they both *should* and *could* be at, if they had been helped more at home.

Moreover, she knew of many parents who were abusing alcohol and drugs. And the parents of one of her children had been reported the previous year to the Department of Children and Families for suspected child abuse. The investigation had been inconclusive, but the family was receiving social services. Theresa was concerned that a few other children in the class might be experiencing abuse at home, but she didn't have enough evidence to act on.

Still, she knew that many families were caught up in just meeting their basic needs for survival, so whenever she could, she expressed appreciation to the parents. Under her guidance, the children made cards for every possible holiday and thanked the parents and other family members for their help. In the notebooks, Theresa periodically thanked each parent—whether she genuinely felt they were helping or not.

Summing up her feelings, Theresa remarked, "I realize that what makes me so frustrated is that I need to keep on top of the parents as much as the kids."

Discussion Questions

1. In general, what types of family involvement are there? Which ones do you see in this case?
2. How might the situation appear from the parents' perspective? From the children's perspective?
3. How might Theresa's own background be affecting her attitude?

4. Should Theresa have changed her strategies? If so, why, at what point, and how?
   • Is she expecting too much of the children, the parents, and herself?
5. If you were Theresa, what would you do now?
   • Is she at risk of burnout? If so, how could she avoid it?
6. What other strategies, if any, might she try?
7. Is family involvement within the school building a realistic or useful goal in this situation?
   • Should Theresa try to connect families with social services?
   • What other resources might she draw upon in the school and community?

Suggested Activities

1. Interview a principal or a teacher in an urban school that has involved families. Identify what strategies were used and which ones were most successful. What problems arose in encouraging family involvement? What does the principal perceive as the benefits of family involvement for the children?
2. Role-play a telephone conversation between Theresa and a parent who Theresa is encouraging to become more involved in helping her child with homework. Enact the situation twice, exchanging roles so that you gain an understanding of both the teacher's and parent's perspectives.
3. Research and write a paper on various types of family involvement. Compare these strategies to those Theresa tried.

How Much Parent Involvement Is Too Much?

CHARACTERS

Principals:	George Berman
	Jeffrey Dixon
Teachers:	John Braverman
	Marjory Coleman
School psychologist:	Muriel Bender
Assistant Superintendent	
of Curriculum:	Marsha Dillard
Staff Developer:	Mark Davis
Parent:	Joseph Gordon

George Berman, the principal at Sachem School, had been working with an advisory committee of parents for a couple of years to reform the school's fifth- and sixth-grade curriculum. They were just beginning to come to grips with what they really wanted. To make sure the entire parent body was fully informed about various curriculum approaches, George had asked two well-respected teachers to conduct a workshop, which would focus on the advantages and disadvantages of a subject-based approach versus an integrated curriculum. The two teachers met several times to plan their presentation.

On the evening of the workshop, about 50 parents gathered in the gym. Never expecting so many, George and the committee were delighted. After people helped themselves to dessert and chatted for a while, the teachers began their presentation.

Just as they were finishing, Joseph Gordon stood up. A tall, formidable presence, he towered over the group. He pointed at George and thundered, "You people are getting the wool pulled over your eyes. . . . He's making a farce out of the whole curriculum subcommittee!"

George couldn't believe his ears.

THE SCHOOL, COMMUNITY, AND PRINCIPAL

Newport was a suburb of the state's largest city and had approximately 30,000 middle-class and upper-middle-class residents of diverse racial and ethnic backgrounds. Their homes were large, with well-manicured lawns and intriguing play structures for their children. Many of the parents worked at the two large scientific companies headquartered in the area.

Newport had four elementary schools, a junior high school, and a senior high school. Sachem School was the largest of the elementary schools. Its sprawling one-story modern structure housed three classrooms at every grade level from kindergarten through sixth grade. It had many specialists, including a school psychologist, two special education teachers, and full-time art and music teachers. There was even an indoor swimming pool that was used as a community pool after school hours.

Although the schools had received strong support from the community in the past, in the last few years the town had started to tighten its financial belt. The community's population was growing older. Many of the residents' children had graduated from the school system, and now these older residents were less willing to approve bond issues needed for sustaining the system's excellence.

The teachers at Sachem were primarily veterans who took pride in offering a stimulating curriculum that still focused on developing basic academic skills. Although the teachers tended to work independently, they occasionally shared an idea or activity with each other.

The fundamentals of the curriculum had not been seriously reevaluated for several years. For the most part, especially in the higher grades, teachers taught each subject separately. There were clearly defined times for reading and language arts, math, science, and social studies instruction.

Recently, some teachers had become interested in an integrated approach to the curriculum, in which children studied a key concept or theme, and subject areas were integrated within this topic as much as possible. They had read professional literature expounding the benefits of this approach and knew it was being tried in some of the new middle schools in neighboring districts. But other teachers saw no need for change. They reasoned that the children scored extremely well in national standardized tests, so why fix something if it's not broken?

In the past five years, as part of a national trend, family involvement had been increasingly encouraged at Sachem School. The parents helped in a variety of ways: volunteering in classrooms, tutoring children, carrying out projects, and chaperoning field trips.

Each year, the Parent-Teacher Organization (PTO) raised a substantial amount of money. Two years earlier, it provided the school with one of the largest and most attractive playgrounds in the area. The school's extensive computer facility was another benefit of the parents' fund-raising.

Parents also served in an advisory capacity to the school. The PTO's monthly gathering included standing committee meetings, as well as an open meeting for parents, teachers, and other school staff. Committees focused on areas such as the budget, fund-raising, the curriculum, personnel, and advocacy for the school at the Board of Education meetings.

This was George Berman's first year as principal of Sachem School. He had taught for 10 years at an elementary school in a nearby town and had a reputation as a creative, innovative teacher. A year earlier, he had received an advanced degree in administration and supervision from a prestigious university. He then landed a job as assistant principal at Sachem School and was eager to learn the ropes of administration.

During that year, the principal, Jeffrey Dixon, became ill and announced that he would retire. George was chosen as his successor. Retiring after a productive 30-year career, Jeffrey had been beloved by students, teachers, and parents alike. Although he was stern and kept a tight rein on the school, he was also respected as fair and principled.

THE PTO MEETING

In September, George looked forward to the PTO meeting, his first such meeting as a new principal. He eagerly undertook the challenge of working with this group of energetic, knowledgeable parents. Typically, the standing committees met in small groups and then there was a general meeting.

As George rotated among the standing committees, he overheard some heated discussion coming from the Curriculum Committee. The committee was questioning the content and delivery of the fifth- and sixth-grade curricula. They particularly questioned whether there was adequate attention given to math and science instruction and whether these subjects were taught with enough depth to be meaningful to the students. Just below the surface there seemed to be an unstated concern about whether the teachers were even adequately prepared to teach these subjects.

This was an area of intense interest to many of the parents. Several parents on the committee were themselves scientists, working in the research and development centers of the large chemical companies in the area. Entering into the discussion, George suggested that they might want to form a subcommittee to focus solely on the fifth-and sixth-grade curricula. He expected four or five parents to join it.

During the course of the evening, other subcommittees were formed as well. At one point, Muriel Bender, the school psychologist, took him aside. From the wellspring of her 20 years' experience working with parents, Muriel counseled George. "You know, you might be going a bit too fast. I know you want to try new things, branch out, but I'm getting nervous. Don't you think you should hold on tighter to the reins?"

But George was consciously letting go of the reins because he wanted to see where the process would lead. "I was following on the heels of a principal who maintained tight control," he said later, "and my personal style was different. At its best this was risk-taking, but maybe I just wasn't experienced enough to know how to say no."

Furthermore, George had a special interest in the fifth- and sixth-grade levels. He had taught mostly at these levels himself. He had a gnawing feeling that math and science instruction was being neglected, and that kids weren't entering the junior high as well prepared as they might be.

He was also intrigued by the increased focus on integrated curriculum in the professional literature. It was seen as a holistic way of teaching that mirrored the real world. After all, the everyday world wasn't separated into distinct disciplines. An integrated curriculum could help children to see real-world applications for new information, improve retention by showing them how facts interrelate, and motivate them to learn more. In addition, this type of curriculum fostered collaboration among teachers.

At the next meeting of the PTO, George was bowled over to see that 25 parents had joined the curriculum subcommittee. "I felt very supported and excited that I had all these people fighting to make our curriculum stronger," he remembered. "The parents wanted a more cohesive, stimulating program for the older students, and so did I. I thought I could use parent power to achieve it."

He gave them his blessings with one important caveat: he stated clearly that the final decision about the nature of the program would be his. Those kinds of decisions were his responsibility as a principal and were what he got paid for. He recalled deliberately repeating this several times to the parents over the long period that they eventually worked on this project.

Then, something happened to halt the progress. John Braverman, a sixth-grade teacher, quit. His wife had landed a new job in another state, and the family was moving. A member of the subcommittee, John had provided a seasoned teacher's input into the parents' deliberations. Although two other teachers remained on the committee, they were younger and less experienced.

"Now, just when everyone was motivated and we were developing some momentum, things slowed down," George said.

THE SECOND YEAR

George realized that the parents on the subcommittee were starting to get very frustrated. "I felt I needed to tap their energy," he said, "because it was beginning to fester."

Moreover, he could really use their help. He was writing the budget and had to justify his request for a staff developer to help redesign the curriculum and train teachers, with a focus on the higher levels. To draw on the parents' expertise and show he valued their efforts, he asked the parents on the sub-committee to participate in three ways:

1. to write and sign a rationale to be attached to the budget, with the understanding that he might yea or nay their draft;
2. to develop and send a survey to the entire parent body to generate interest in curriculum issues and to assess other parents' wishes;
3. to help interview candidates for the staff developer position, if and when the time came.

"I felt good about my request," George said. "It was focused, respectful, and useful to the students, teachers, and me."

THE RATIONALE

The subcommittee asked Joseph Gordon to write the rationale. Joseph was a chemist who worked at the research facility of a large scientific concern. Brilliant and volatile, his eyes sparkled when he talked about his field. He seemed to George to be an articulate, knowledgeable spokesperson.

Joseph's rationale was strong and persuasive. It focused on the importance of reforming the curriculum to prepare students for the demands of an increasingly technological society in the 21st century. It emphasized a strong subject-based approach to math and science instruction. It envisioned students working in state-of-the-art laboratories conducting science experiments as real scientists would. In mathematics, students would be pushed to the highest levels that they could master.

George was impressed by the rationale. He thought that Joseph was using subject-based math and science instruction as an example of the benefits of curriculum reform and that the plan was flexible. When he presented the budget, this rationale would serve to ignite the Board's interest and support. Later, the plan could be modified as the school wished.

"Maybe, because I was busy or naive, I didn't read the rationale as carefully as I should have," George commented in retrospect.

THE SURVEY

As George requested, the subcommittee designed and administered a survey on curriculum to the parents. It asked the parents to identify what they considered to be the strengths and weaknesses of the current fifth- and sixth-grade curricula. The results showed that there was a great deal of parent interest in improving math and science instruction but no agreement as to the approach that should be adopted.

Although it was valuable, George did not think the survey should determine the course of the curriculum. He told the subcommittee that he saw the results as one part of the puzzle. The survey was not statistically valid or reliable, but it was useful information.

OTHER EFFORTS

The subcommittee also worked with the school system's assistant superintendent for curriculum, Marsha Dillard. Marsha was impressed by their verve and determination to get a staff developer for Sachem School. Although she was extremely busy, she met with the parents several times, which, George later speculated, must have been empowering for them.

Marsha agreed to go to bat for Sachem and support its request to the Board at its spring meeting. George was elated. The more support for a budget request a school had, the more likely it was to be approved. Now, Marsha, the parents, and George were all fighting to redesign the curriculum.

MAKING PROGRESS

At the Board meeting in April, George presented the budget and read Joseph's rationale. Everyone was thrilled when the request for the staff development position was approved. George remembered telephoning four or five members of the subcommittee to cheer, "We did it!"

INTERVIEWING THE CANDIDATES

Next, George convened a committee to interview candidates for the position. The committee included Joseph, as well as four other members of the personnel committee. They interviewed eight candidates and unanimously chose Mark Davis. Mark was experienced and widely recognized as a talented teacher. Moreover, he had recently completed a sixth-year professional diploma, with a specialty in curriculum design.

George remembered that Joseph played a positive role in the interviewing process. One of the candidates happened to be the parent of a child in the school, but she was not the committee's first choice. This was potentially a sticky situation and George commented, "It was helpful to have Joseph, another parent, say to her, 'No, we're sorry'."

In the fall, Sachem School would have a staff developer. Mark enthusiastically offered to begin work on a curriculum during the summer, to propose to George and the subcommittee in the fall.

THE SUBCOMMITTEE MEETS

In late April, the curriculum subcommittee met again. For the first time, George sensed a division within the group. Now that curriculum reform was being supported by the Board, there was disagreement as to what *kind* of reform. The parents started bickering among themselves.

Some parents, with Joseph in the lead, were stalwart supporters of subject-based instruction, with a stronger emphasis on math and science. Other committee members agreed that the math and science instruction needed to be beefed up, but they saw benefits in an integrated approach to curriculum. Advocates of a subject-based approach argued that an integrated approach would water down the content of the subject areas and make it harder for teachers to cover all of their curriculum objectives.

George remembered thinking, "Something's backfiring here and I'm not sure what it is. But I'll probably end up taking the brunt of it." He saw that the split in the committee would make *any* decision he made likely to displease *some* of the parents, who seemed to be split about 50–50 on the issue.

He reminded the subcommittee that, while he valued their input, ultimately he would make the final decision. In making the decision, he assured them that he would take into account the goals of the school, the needs and interests of the students, the strengths of the teachers, and the parents' wishes.

He reminded the parents that fifth and sixth graders were *not* at the same cognitive level as high school students and might not be able to handle material at the same level of sophistication. Moreover, he noted that there was a growing trend to integrate the curriculum at the middle school level.

As the meeting was coming to an end, Joseph stood up. His face was beet red. "I want your decision now! We've been working on this for months. We don't want an integrated curriculum. What about the rationale to the Board? We have a commitment to that!" he stormed.

George was stunned. No parent had ever shouted him down before! He felt that Joseph was engaging in a personal power play with him and presuming to speak for the whole group. But there was clearly a strong division among the parents over the kind of curriculum they favored.

Moreover, he recognized that perhaps several of the parents felt that he *was* behaving in an underhanded way. It may have seemed that, after all of their hard work to get the position approved, he was going to take the ball and run with it. Maybe he planned to follow his own agenda, with little regard for theirs.

Trying to stay calm, he explained that he needed to deliberate carefully about such a major decision. He would inform them of his decision when they met again in a few weeks. He expressed great appreciation for the committee's energetic efforts. Between now and then, he felt it would be helpful if members of the teaching staff provided a workshop for the entire parent body on various approaches to curriculum design to further inform everyone.

THE WORKSHOP

George asked two veteran teachers, one from fifth grade and one from sixth grade, to lead a workshop on different approaches to curriculum design, focusing particularly on the advantages and disadvantages of both an integrated approach and a subject-based approach.

The teachers were delighted with the opportunity to share their expertise with the parents. They spent hours planning an instructive evening. One, Marjory Coleman, had never conducted such a workshop, and George realized that it was a good opportunity for her to grow professionally. George arranged to have some pastries and coffee for the gathering.

The workshop was held in late May. Fifty parents came, far more than the staff expected. First the parents mingled sociably and enjoyed the food. Then, from George's perspective, the two teachers gave an informative, impartial presentation on various approaches to curriculum design. George was feeling very pleased, and the workshop was about to end.

All of a sudden, Joseph stood up. "You people are getting the wool pulled over your eyes," he exploded. "The curriculum subcommittee made a decision about the program, and now your principal is unilaterally changing our plans. He signed this rationale and now he's backing down on it." He started furiously passing out the rationale.

Joseph's face was flushed as he pointed at George and charged, "He's making a farce out of the whole curriculum subcommittee!"

Discussion Questions

1. What is the immediate problem that George faces?
2. What are the underlying issues in this situation?
3. How did this situation develop?
   - Consider George's administrative style.
   - Were the parents taking advantage of a novice principal?
4. Could this situation have been avoided? If so, how?
   - Should George have sensed problems brewing sooner? Were there any indicators? If so, what were they?
   - Was Muriel right that George should hold on tighter to the reins? What are the potential losses to a school if a principal holds the reins too tightly?
   - What role should the teachers have in this situation?
5. In this case, was there too much parent involvement? How much parent involvement is too much?
   - What are the advantages of parent involvement, as seen in this case?
   - What are possible disadvantages?
   - Could teachers also face decision-making conflicts with parents who volunteer in the classroom?

6. Should parents advise on curriculum issues? If so, how much authority should they have?
7. Should administrators and teachers define clear boundaries between parents' roles and responsibilities in a school and the professionals' roles and responsibilities?
    • Where are the proper boundaries? Might they differ from school to school?
    • How should boundaries be established? Who should establish them?
8. How should George respond to Joseph at the end of the case?
    • What factors does he need to consider?
9. If you were George, what would you do now about reforming the curriculum at Sachem School?

Suggested Activities

1. Role-play the scene at the end of the case, with two people enacting the roles of George and Joseph. Then reverse roles, so the role-players can gain an understanding of the other perspective. The rest of the class can be the other parents at the meeting. Through the role play, consider possible ways that George might handle this difficult situation.
2. Visit a school that encourages family involvement and interview an administrator. In what ways are parents involved in the school? Which ways have been most useful to the school? Have any problems arisen? If so, how have they been handled?
3. Imagine you are a teacher who wishes to encourage parent involvement in your classroom. What guidelines for parents might you develop to avoid potential problems? What kinds of interaction would be helpful to both parents and teachers?

Multicultural Misunderstanding

CHARACTERS

Principal:	Anita Reinhardt
Parents:	Henry Stevens
	Jane Farrar

Anita Reinhardt, the principal at Lakeview Elementary School, was meeting with a school standing committee examining school goals. They were discussing how Lakeview's multicultural program related to a new state law that required every town to develop a voluntary regional desegregation plan. It was a few months after the school's first Multicultural Day, which had focused on African culture through the arts and had seemed highly successful.

Then, Henry Stevens, one of the parents on the committee, spoke up. The treasurer of the Parent-Teacher Association and a pillar of the community, Henry was a pharmacist whose family had run a drugstore in the center of the small town for two generations. He had four children, at both the elementary and middle schools, and both he and his wife were actively involved in their schools.

Henry's comments bowled Anita over.

"I hope the Multicultural Committee isn't planning one of *those* programs again this year," he asserted.

Anita was taken aback. "What do you mean?" she asked.

THE SCHOOL, COMMUNITY, AND PRINCIPAL

A sleek, modern structure, Lakeview Elementary School was constructed five years earlier. It was the first new school built in the town of Woodstock in 25 years, and the community was justifiably proud of its physical plant. It had an indoor pool, a well-equipped media center, a spectacular gymnasium, computer equipment in each classroom, and windows that looked out on landscaped grounds. Of the approximately 600 students in the kindergarten through the fifth grade, about 99 percent were white. The teachers were all white women.

The PTA at Lakeview was an active, dynamic group. In fact, the school staff had begun to rely on it as a major source of funds because it raised $25,000–30,000 a year. The school had recently used most of the year's funds to build a beautiful new playground structure. The library also received $1,000.

Woodstock was a small town. Most of the families were middle to upper middle class, and many parents worked in the several corporations that had moved to the area. There were, however, some working class and low income families. Several trailer parks bordered the town, and a few homeless families, who were subsidized by the state, lived in motels.

Woodstock was located about 15 miles from Winchester, a city of 190,000. Winchester's population was about one-third white, one-third African-American, and one-third Hispanic. Winchester was a rich cultural resource for the entire county. Its dance company and repertory theater were renowned in the area. Moreover, it provided state-of-the-art medical care through its three hospitals. Winchester had more than its share of urban problems, including unemployment, poverty, violence, and drug trafficking. Real estate prices had plummeted in the last five years, and many houses sported "For Sale" signs. A recent study warned that Winchester's children fared worse than the state's children in general, since the city had far higher rates of poor prenatal care, infant mortality, teenage mothers, child deaths, and high school dropouts.

In the state itself, a landmark court case was in progress. A group of parents from the capital city of Benton were suing the state. They claimed that their children were not receiving an equitable education because of de facto economic and racial segregation due to residential patterns. These parents were seeking a court order requiring the metropolitan region to develop a plan to integrate the capital and suburban schools. (The city schools served primarily minority children.)

In an attempt to avoid court-ordered desegregation, the state passed a law requiring regional school districts to develop voluntary desegregation plans. Although the districts were mandated to develop a plan, once developed, the communities had a choice of either adopting or rejecting the implementation of the plan.

Anita Reinhardt had been the principal at Lakeview for five years, after teaching for many years at the elementary level in town. She was 57 years old and lived in Woodstock. Her husband was a lawyer, and they had two grown children.

She had grown up in modest circumstances in the city of Winchester. One of seven children, she had attended school with children from a variety of ethnic and racial backgrounds and valued that experience. Her father, an upholsterer who worked in a factory, was periodically laid off from work, and Anita remembered those hard times. Sometimes the electricity was cut off or there wasn't much to eat. The family was nonetheless close and caring, and both parents made the children feel rich in love.

Energetic and enthusiastic, Anita enjoyed her work. As Lakeview's first principal, her main concern five years before had been to help the students and staff adjust to their new school. Both teachers and students had been funneled from two other elementary schools in different parts of town and needed to get to know each other and learn to work together.

THE OTHER PARENT

Jane Farrar, a vivacious woman in her late 30's, had three children, ages 10, seven, and five, in the Woodstock school system. She and her husband, a social worker, had moved to Woodstock from Winchester about eight years previously.

A teacher as well as a parent, Jane had spent her entire career teaching English at the high school level in nearby Winchester. Having received numerous awards, she was well known as a caring, demanding, and innovative teacher. She frequently took advantage of opportunities at Winchester's universities to update her skills in new teaching strategies or in her specialty.

Jane taught at a magnet school whose special focus was the arts. There were resident artists on staff to teach dance, music, drama, and visual arts to the students. The regular teachers often collaborated to create interdisciplinary units, which might combine literature and history, as well as the arts, from a particular period.

Jane's school had an enrollment of about 300 students, of whom 85 percent were African-American, 14 percent were Hispanic, and about 1 percent were Caucasian. The students were primarily from low income backgrounds.

THE STORY BEGINS

Since her own children had begun school, Jane had seen little evidence of a multicultural curriculum in their classes beyond the occasional lessons on Native American cultures, especially around Thanksgiving, and the observance of the birthday of Martin Luther King, Jr. She had regularly attended PTA meetings, and the subject of multiculturalism had never come up there either.

When Jeffrey, her fifth grader, was in second grade, she decided to ask the principal about the multicultural program. Anita Reinhardt assured her that all of the teachers were doing "something" in that area. That year, Jane still didn't see much.

The next year, Jane asked Mrs. Reinhardt to report to the PTA on aspects of the multicultural curriculum. Perhaps the teachers could describe projects or studies that the children had done. "I was sure some things were going on in this area. Maybe Jeffrey was just missing it in the classes he had been in," she commented to a friend. She knew that the cultural arts committee was looking for programs to bring to the school that year.

Mrs. Reinhardt agreed to report to the PTA but never did. By the end of the year, Jane had asked about the multicultural curriculum several times. She was always reassured and then gently put off.

In April of that year, the steering committee of the PTA announced in the school newsletter that it would hold elections at the June PTA meeting. Any parent could volunteer to be an officer. Moreover, they had created a multicultural committee to bring multicultural education to the school. Because that meeting was held on the night that her own students graduated, Jane could not attend.

Then, in early July, Jane ran into another parent in the supermarket who congratulated her on winning the election to chair the multicultural committee. Jane was dumbfounded. She had not nominated herself for the position, but she reflected later, "I've learned that if you ask a question, you'll be put in charge."

The results of the election, as well as the budget allotment for each committee, were announced in the summer edition of the school newsletter. Jane was bemused to see that the multicultural committee was scheduled to receive the grand sum of $100.00. Trying to be positive, she called the president of the PTA to say that she was happy to chair the committee. The president reassured her that the budget was flexible, and that more monies could be made available.

"Who else signed up for the committee?" Jane asked. "No one, but why don't you announce a need for members in the next newsletter?" the president responded.

DESIGNING A MULTICULTURAL PROGRAM

In mid-August, Jane set up a meeting with the principal. The staff and students were now well adjusted to the five-year-old school, and Anita could shift her focus. She was eager to incorporate multicultural education into the program.

Jane was full of ideas but had limited time and energy since she was working full-time. She knew she had to "work small but carefully." She decided to make some suggestions to the principal, let her pick one or two, and then gather together a committee.

Jane's first thought was an International Fair, which she knew other schools had held. Each class chose an area of the world to study and represent. Students learned about their own heritage, and parents from various ethnic groups could participate by wearing ethnic clothing or sharing artifacts. In Lakeview's case, families were mainly from Italian, French, and Irish backgrounds.

This idea didn't appeal to Anita. "Our students do need to learn about their own heritage, but they can do it on a smaller scale within their classrooms. And I want them to learn more than just research skills," she told Jane. Instead, she felt that the students would benefit most from active involvement and one-to-one interaction with people from racial and cultural backgrounds to which they'd had little or no exposure.

Jane was secretly pleased. She had been mulling over another idea but was uncertain how it would be received. She decided to propose it. She suggested an all-day event to build awareness of African culture. Her students from the creative arts magnet high school could come to Lakeview to perform a drama piece, interweaving dance and music. Both high school and elementary students would eat lunch together. Then, in the afternoon, the high school students would go back to the classrooms with the children to assist in a visual arts project. Parent volunteers would be tapped to help the teachers with the project. The day could be held in February, during Black History Month.

Anita Reinhardt was delighted. This was just the sort of real opportunity to interact with people from other backgrounds that she wanted for her students. She urged Jane to begin work on the project. As a teacher at an urban school with a diverse population of students and a parent of a child at a suburban school with a homogenous student body, Jane was in a position to bridge both worlds.

Recruiting Supporters in Woodstock and Winchester

Jane first met with the head of the arts department at her high school. "I think this is a great opportunity," he responded. "We need more urban-suburban programs and maybe young children will appreciate our performers more than their fellow students do. High school students can be pretty rough on each other."

Together, they contacted theatre, dance, and visual arts teachers on the staff. Jane met with each of them to brainstorm ideas and set a date.

In Woodstock, Jane's effort to recruit volunteers at Lakeview school to help her in the overall planning was virtually futile. Only two parents offered to help, and neither was very available.

She also needed parents to volunteer to work on the day of the event, assisting with the African art project in the classes. She and the head of the Parent Volunteers Committee ended up calling 80 parents. Of those, 50 agreed to help out that day, with two to three parents per classroom.

Laying the Groundwork

Jane carefully organized the event. With the staff from her school, she identified 25 high school students to be involved. The group included five Latino students, five white students, and 15 African-American students. All of these students had been in Jane's classes at one point or another.

She worked with a modest budget. The total program cost $600.00, including art supplies, the bus to bring the high school students to the school, and a modest honorarium for each of the artist-teachers from the high school.

The program would include a morning dramatic presentation and two different afternoon art projects, one for the younger children and one for the older children. The children would create Adinkra designs, symbols of happiness in the home and harmony in the community for the Ashanti people of Ghana. The younger students would make crayon resist drawings, and the older students would be printing the Adinkra symbols on muslin cloth.

The preparation was enormously time-consuming. After the art teacher from her high school told her what materials were needed, Jane proceeded to collect them. "I had almost no help," she said.

For the printmaking, Jane asked a supermarket to donate 50 styrofoam meat trays which she cut into squares. She purchased material from a fabric store and gallons of black paint from a paint store. Her own children helped her to set up a box of supplies for every teacher. At one point, she had 25 supply boxes piled up in her dining room, waiting to be delivered.

A month before the event, Jane hung a poster in the teachers' room describing Adinkra designs to inform the teachers. She also copied the Adinkra charts so that each teacher would have one in the classroom. Moreover, she provided detailed written lesson plans for the teachers and ensured that there would be two or three adults helping in each class.

"I didn't want to do something and not have it go well," she stated. But some teachers never even read the lesson plan. Jane realized that she was walking a fine line as a fellow teacher. "I didn't want to tell these teachers how to teach," she remarked to a colleague.

The Principal's Efforts

Two weeks before the event, Anita sent the teachers a memo informing them of the Multicultural Day and telling them when their students were scheduled to participate. She made clear that everyone was expected to take part.

Juggling the day's schedule to accommodate the program was very complicated. The lunch schedule had to be rearranged to allow for two performances before lunch. Anita provided the funding for the high school students' lunches and ensured that extra tables were set up in the lunchroom.

She also worked hard on the day of the event to ensure that everything went well and to smooth over any problems. She posted a huge welcome sign and encouraged her students to mingle with the guests, so that everyone could get to know each other. When it became clear that more tables and chairs were needed in the cafeteria, she recruited the custodians to bring them in. She made sure that the guests were served lunch in a timely fashion and generally oversaw the running of the day.

THE MULTICULTURAL DAY

The day seemed to go flawlessly. At the request of the mayor, the local cable TV station videotaped the program and aired it. The responses that day and for several months to come were uniformly positive.

The principal was practically dancing with delight. "She was on her toes all day," said Jane. She felt that there had been genuine rapport between her students and the high school students, who were from very different backgrounds. The children were seeing these students in a light that generally wasn't reported in the news.

The elementary school children were dancing, too. They didn't hesitate to come up after the performance to learn the steps from the high school students. They even asked the teenagers for their autographs. Parents commented that weeks later their children were still demonstrating the dance steps they'd learned.

Flattered and touched by the response, the high school students asked to return. One student referred to the little kids as a "kind audience." "They were really watching us and really listening to us." It made them proud to be in the spotlight as performers—and they were teachers as well. They were impressed by the school's physical beauty.

The teachers realized how much time Jane had devoted to the day and expressed their appreciation to her. Many commented on how talented, disciplined, and caring the high school students were. Some even requested follow-up activities, which Jane provided.

One third-grade teacher was so excited that she had her students write letters to the dancers and the characters in the play. A set of 24 letters was sent to Jane's students, asking questions like, "How did you learn to act?" and "Will you come back?" Because many of the high school students responded, there was an unexpected letter exchange.

THE AX FALLS

Jane saw the day as the first step in a five-year plan. Each year, she hoped to have an entire day with a multicultural focus. Next year's celebration would be a Hispanic day.

However, she was exhausted from the experience. Although willing to continue to work on the project, she hoped another parent would assume the chairpersonship of the committee. One parent started to identify resources, but she had young children and didn't want to be chairperson. When elections rolled around, Jane was reelected.

Multicultural education had become a pressing townwide issue. It was part of a larger question of whether the community would vote to approve the regional desegregation plan that had been developed. Anita was strongly in favor of this plan, as was the superintendent of schools.

A school standing committee (representing parents, teachers, and the administration) was responsible for examining school goals and was considering multicultural education in light of regional plans. The committee met with Anita to discuss what the school's multicultural curriculum consisted of and whether it complied with the superintendent's directives and plan for action for the town.

It was at that meeting that Henry Stevens, one of the parents on the standing committee, voiced strong concern. "I hope the Multicultural Committee isn't planning one of *those* programs again this year."

Anita was startled. Well respected in the town, Henry was very active on the PTA as well as numerous other community activities. Energetic and convivial, he coached the Little League and served on the town's library committee. With his power and influence in the community, Henry's opinion was not to be taken lightly. "What do you mean?" Anita asked.

"It was just such a limited program," Henry said. "The whole focus was on Africa, and now I've heard that Jane is planning a Hispanic day. I don't know why she's calling that committee a multicultural committee. Why doesn't she just call it a Black and Puerto Rican Committee?"

He paused pointedly and then continued. "I'm not sure it even makes sense to bring those high school kids in from the city to be with our children. And I'm not the only parent who feels this way. I wonder if most of the teachers even back this."

Anita's face was flushed. She struggled to compose a response.

Discussion Questions

1. What is Anita Reinhardt's immediate problem in this meeting?
2. What are the underlying issues in this case?
3. Evaluate the multicultural program from the perspectives of the Woodstock and Winchester students, the teachers, the parents, and the administration.
4. How effectively did Anita lay the groundwork to gain support for the multicultural program before the multicultural day?
5. What might Anita have done after the multicultural day to ensure ongoing support for the program?
6. Evaluate Jane's role.
   • Should she have done anything differently?
7. Should parents have a major influence on a school's curriculum?
   • What are the possible advantages of parent involvement in curriculum issues?
   • What are the possible disadvantages?
8. How should Anita respond to Henry Stevens at the end of the case?
   • What further actions should she take?

Suggested Activities

1. Role-play the discussion between Henry Stevens and Anita Reinhardt at the standing committee meeting. Switch roles so that you can experience both participants' perspectives. Through the role-play, consider possible ways that Anita might handle this situation.

2. Visit a school that encourages active parent involvement through committees. Interview an administrator to find out how parents working in this capacity have been most useful to the school. Have any problems arisen? If so, how have they been handled? What is the role, if any, of parents in curriculum design? If policies have been established in this area, what are they?

3. Review the literature on multicultural education. What are the range of goals and strategies for achieving multicultural goals? Write a research paper on this topic.

4. Investigate how schools in settings similar to Woodstock incorporate multiculturalism into their curricula.

What's My Role?

CHARACTERS

Kindergarten teacher:	Melissa Anthony
School psychologist:	Edith Morgan
Student:	Callie Lindner
Parents:	Ellen and David Lindner

It was a humid, late-summer day, and Melissa Anthony was busy decorating her kindergarten room for the first day of school tomorrow. By the end of the summer she was always eager to start again, and she looked forward to meeting the children in her class. As she was straightening the puzzles on the shelf, a mother and young girl walked into the room. Melissa's principal had left her a note saying that Mrs. Lindner and her daughter planned to drop by.

"Hi, I'm Mrs. Anthony," Melissa warmly greeted them. Mrs. Lindner introduced herself and her daughter, Callie. Melissa observed that both the mother and the little girl looked uncomfortable, but that certainly was typical when young children started school. Trying to be reassuring, Melissa told Callie some of the things she'd be doing in kindergarten. Callie cast her eyes downward.

"Look at your teacher," her mother admonished her. Callie seemed anxious to leave.

"We just moved here from Dallas," Mrs. Lindner explained. "I tried to contact the social worker over the summer but wasn't able to reach her, so I thought I'd just come in. I wanted to let you know that Callie is a smart little girl but she has a lot of difficulties."

Melissa was taken aback. It shocked her that Mrs. Lindner would make this comment right in front of Callie. She simply nodded in response, to avoid drawing further attention to the remark. Then she gave Callie a quick tour of the classroom and suggested to her, "Now that we know each other, you can be my helper tomorrow."

As Mrs. Lindner and Callie left the room, Melissa mulled over what Mrs. Lindner could have meant by her statement. She wondered what lay in store for her.

THE SCHOOL, COMMUNITY, AND TEACHER

South Freeport Elementary School was sheltered by a bank of beautiful maple trees on a side road in the community of Melton. The school's setting seemed to symbolize the parents' protective caring of their children. Founded in the early 1700s, Melton was a wealthy town with elegant, white clapboard colonial homes and a pristine town square at its center.

The school had about 500 children in its kindergarten through sixth grades. Both the staff and children were predominantly white, and there were only a handful of non-English-speaking children. Like the community, the school was well endowed. Among elementary schools, its media center had one of the largest collections in the state. There was at least one computer in every classroom, and many had more. The school's special education services included a full-time speech-language pathologist, a full-time school psychologist, a full-time social worker, and a resource teacher who worked primarily with children with learning disabilities.

Melissa Anthony had grown up in a neighboring town. Although her parents had not attended college, they valued education. They encouraged their daughter's prolific reading and were very proud when she became the first family member to receive a higher education.

Melissa had a masters degree in early childhood education and had been teaching for seven years. She taught first grade for five years, and this was her second year teaching kindergarten. She loved teaching young children because it lent itself to hands-on experiences such as art, movement, and singing. Moreover, Melissa preferred teaching children who posed a challenge. Although she had to work harder to meet their needs, she felt greater satisfaction when they made progress.

THE CHILD AND FAMILY

David Lindner had been a corporate executive with a Fortune 500 company, and his family had moved many times to accommodate the evolution of his career in the company. The previous June, he had taken an early retirement to start his own business as a consultant. Ellen Lindner was a librarian; she had not yet found a job. The family returned to the Melton area because both parents had attended college there and had liked it. They were renting a house until they found one they wanted to purchase. Callie, at six and a half, was the youngest of five children, although Callie never mentioned her siblings to Melissa. The three older girls seemed to be doing fine in school, but Callie's brother was having difficulty in fifth grade. He was inattentive in class and went home sick a couple of times a week. He had not been identified for special services but was receiving speech therapy for articulation problems.

From what Melissa had seen so far, this seemed to be a family under stress. One evening, Melissa called Ellen Lindner to discuss Callie's day at school. As they talked, Melissa heard Callie screaming in the background. The yelling became louder and louder, and Melissa had the impression that Callie was hurting her mother in some way. Then, she picked up a phone in another room and shouted into it, "I hate you!"

There was dead silence. Melissa was taken aback, and Mrs. Lindner didn't respond to Callie. After a few seconds, Callie hung up the phone. Mrs. Lindner apologized to Melissa for her behavior and then confessed, "If Callie were my first child, I don't know if I would have had any more children." She explained that at home when Callie was angry, she often became violent and kicked and threw objects. She would also lose control when she was happy, and was unable to contain her excitement. Melissa hadn't seen this behavior at school, but she had seen other behavior that distressed her.

Callie was repeating kindergarten. Her previous school had identified her as having special needs and developed an individualized education plan (IEP) for Callie, which she brought to South Freeport. The IEP indicated that she required occupational therapy to improve her small motor coordination. For example, she had difficulty buttoning and zipping her clothes and holding a pencil correctly.

THE BEGINNING OF SCHOOL

On the first day of school, Melissa met her students when the buses arrived, as she would every day. She liked to start the year off right, helping the children to learn the daily routines. As they got off the bus, she lined them up and asked them to wait until everyone was present. When Callie arrived, she remembered her promise to her and put her at the head of the line to lead the group to the classroom. Before she could caution the children to walk slowly, Callie began racing down the halls and the other 17 children chased after her. Melissa hurried behind but couldn't get ahead of them to slow down their pace.

There were new incidents every day. Melissa began to suspect that Callie had Attention Deficit Hyperactivity Disorder (ADHD).

Callie was a child in constant motion. If the class gathered for circle time, she sat with her back to Melissa. Melissa had to remind her over and over to listen and not to chat with or nudge the other children. Callie often ended up in the middle of the circle or stood up and wandered around.

When Callie was supposed to work independently at her table, she was unable to focus for even a few minutes. She'd get up, look in her supply box, and talk to nearby children. Her work area was a mess: papers were scattered everywhere, her coat was on the floor, and her shoes were off. Melissa had given her at least five boxes of crayons labeled with her name, but they still got lost. She seemed incapable of organizing herself for work.

Melissa was particularly disconcerted by the repetitive noises that Callie made. "It's a kind of quacking sound and I don't think she even realizes she does it," she told Edith Morgan, the school psychologist. She also had nervous tics and unusual eye blinking.

At times, Callie's speech was unintelligible and her receptive language seemed poor. She frequently did not understand Melissa's comments or instructions. Melissa felt that Callie *was* listening for the most part, but she didn't seem to process the information.

Melissa had begun to work on letter names and sounds with the children. Callie was able to identify a letter, such as "B," and say its sound in isolation, but she could not then give examples of words that began with that sound. Additionally, if she was given a photocopy showing various objects and was asked to color those beginning with the same sound, she couldn't do it.

Although she could be exhausting, Melissa found Callie likable. "There's a neediness," she said. "She seems to need attention, or love, or someone to listen a little. She comes up to me quite often and just wants to talk." She also found her intelligent. For a six-year-old, her background knowledge was advanced. She was fascinated by dinosaurs and insects and knew all kinds of information about them. Moreover, she had a sophisticated way of thinking and writing about things as well as a good sense of humor.

The other children liked her, too. They enjoyed talking and playing with her. Occasionally, she became wild in her play, throwing blocks for example, and then other children got caught up in the frenzy. Melissa had to be careful to seat her next to children who weren't likely to join her in negative behavior.

Melissa once tried keeping Callie in from recess to discipline her, but that didn't seem to bother her. "I hate to punish her," she said, "because I don't think it will teach her a lesson. I think a lot of this behavior is out of her control."

After a week of working with Callie and after reviewing her permanent record, Melissa decided that she needed to consult with other colleagues. She asked the social worker, school psychologist, principal, and speech-language pathologist to observe Callie in the classroom. After observing Callie and reading her record, all agreed that more information was necessary. They arranged for the Planning and Placement Team (PPT) to meet with Callie's parents at the end of September. Perhaps the Lindners could suggest ways of helping their daughter; for their part, the school professionals intended to recommend that Callie be given a full evaluation.

Meanwhile, Melissa wrote notes to the Lindners and called about once a week to keep them informed. When she described Callie's behaviors, Mrs. Lindner almost seemed to commiserate with her. She explained that she saw the same behaviors, if not worse, at home. However, Melissa noted that although Mrs. Lindner wanted to know what could be done to help Callie, she was focused on what the *school* could do, not what they could do at home.

THE PLANNING AND PLACEMENT TEAM MEETING

At the meeting of the Planning and Placement Team in late September, the Lindners agreed to a full evaluation for Callie. The previous year, they had taken Callie to a neurologist for a battery of tests, but nothing had been found. They seemed eager to get to the source of Callie's problems.

Although Callie had entered South Freeport with an individualized education plan from another state authorizing occupational therapy (OT) for her, she was still not receiving these services. When a child needed OT for small motor problems, this school system preferred to let the resource teacher help the child whenever possible to avoid the cost of hiring an occupational therapist. The PPT decided to await the results of the evaluation to determine whether the resource teacher could handle Callie's OT needs.

At this meeting, Melissa met David Lindner for the first time, and found him quite pleasant. He mentioned that there was a history of learning disabilities in the family. Mr. and Mrs. Lindner occasionally corrected each other's comments, and at one point, Mrs. Lindner testily countered, "I'm sure I remember what happened that time better than you do!" Melissa felt sympathy for the Lindners, who semed to be under considerable stress.

CAUGHT IN THE MIDDLE

After the PPT, Melissa continued to maintain contact with Mrs. Lindner. She didn't see or hear from Mr. Lindner again. By early November, Melissa had twice chatted with Mrs. Lindner when she picked Callie up from school. On one of those days, Mrs. Lindner seemed to blame herself for Callie's behavior. "I've been yelling a lot lately," she confessed to Melissa.

Melissa called Callie's home two times just to touch base and to let the Lindners know how Callie was doing generally. She felt that it would be pointless to call to discuss specific incidents, since there were 20 of those a day. Melissa found that Mrs. Lindner listened but didn't say much, except to acknowledge, "We see the same things, only worse." Melissa also sent some notes to the Lindners.

Melissa occasionally suggested ways that the Lindners might help teach Callie personal skills, such as how to tie her shoes or zip up her coat, but apparently they didn't follow those suggestions. She received no response to the notes she sent home. She would send them homework to do with Callie, but they never returned it.

Although the Lindners said they wanted help themselves and talked about wanting to help Callie, Melissa saw almost no follow-through or action by them. She speculated that the family situation might not be very stable.

By mid-November, Melissa was feeling very frustrated. Although Callie had come to the school with an IEP stipulating occupational therapy for her, she still was not receiving it. The school officials stated that they were in the process of testing to see if the resource teacher could provide the OT.

There had been little action taken on the recommendations from the PPT in late September. Callie needed a battery of tests from the speech-language pathologist, the resource teacher, the school psychologist, the physical education teacher, and an occupational therapist. Someone would come to conduct tests one day, and then no one would return for a week or two. It seemed to be taking a very long time to complete the battery.

Callie had started to receive speech therapy but no language therapy. "The speech-language clinician says she's 'extremely low,' whatever that means," Melissa confided to her husband.

"I'm looking for help from the specialists," Melissa continued with exasperation. "I feel that I'm doing everything I know to do, but it's not enough. It's hard to conduct a lesson and also keep intercepting Callie's behavior. It's rough on Callie, and it's stressful for me. I feel that we're losing time with Callie, and the other children's education is being neglected because she requires so much attention."

WHO'S OBLIGATED TO DO WHAT?

Callie's referral form stated that the PPT would reconvene in late fall to review Callie's test results. Edith Morgan, the school psychologist and head of the PPT team, told Melissa that they would finish the testing by mid-December, but Melissa was outraged by this. "Then half the year's gone by," she complained to her husband. She felt like she was impatiently tapping her foot, waiting for people to finally fulfill their responsibilities.

In late October, Mrs. Lindner contacted Melissa to ask her what kind of services Callie was receiving. Melissa explained that Callie was receiving speech services and that testing was being done to determine whether OT services could be handled by the resource teacher. She then referred Mrs. Lindner to Edith Morgan. She said that she would let Mrs. Morgan and the principal know that Mrs. Lindner had called. Privately, Melissa was delighted that Mrs. Lindner was calling.

Unfortunately, Mrs. Lindner never contacted Edith Morgan. Soon after the phone call, Melissa was leaving in the afternoon when she noticed Mrs. Lindner getting into her car. Melissa caught the mother's eye, but Mrs. Lindner averted her gaze. Mrs. Lindner was clearly avoiding her.

"I feel like I'm caught in the middle," she told her husband. "I'd like to tell the parents that they need to get into school and push. They need to be advocates. But, if I do that, I'm kind of stabbing my colleagues in the back by implying that they're not doing their jobs. I don't even feel that they're not doing their jobs; they're professionals and they're good at what they do. But their caseload is packed. Every day I contact one member of the PPT and ask, 'What about Callie Lindner?' They must be sick of hearing from me. I feel like they're avoiding me now.

Then, on the other hand, I don't know what to make of the Lindners. They say they care, but if Callie were my child, I'd be at school pushing for services for her. They seem so distant. I don't know either of them well and I don't know what to make of them, so I'm afraid to urge them to push harder.

"As a teacher, I feel that I should advocate for my students, but that's also their job as parents."

Discussion Questions

1. What immediate problem(s) is Melissa Anthony facing?
2. What are the important underlying issues in this case?
3. The same situation can look quite different from different perspectives. How might this situation appear from the perspectives of Melissa Anthony? Ellen Lindner? David Lindner? Callie? Edith Morgan? The other children in the class?
4. Were there ways that Melissa or other members of the school staff could have given the Lindners more support? How likely are those to have been successful? Consider the Lindners' reaction to the school's efforts thus far.
5. Should Melissa have pushed the Lindners and/or her colleagues harder to act on Callie's behalf?
   • What might have been accomplished?
   • What problems might that have created?
6. Were there other people Melissa might have used as resources to help her? Who might they be and how might they have helped?
7. Callie's needs are not being met. Is anyone "at fault"? Is it useful to assign blame?
8. If you were the teacher, what would your next step be?

Suggested Activities

1. Interview a school social worker or psychologist who works with parents. What strategies has she or he used to help parents face their child's difficulties and get help for the child?
2. Write a research paper on Attention Deficit Hyperactivity Disorder (ADHD). What are the characteristics of this disorder? What are the difficulties in diagnosing the problem? What multidisciplinary approaches and classroom strategies are used to help children with this disorder?
3. Review material and write a paper discussing the legal rights and responsibilities of parents of children with special needs. What are the specific implications of those rights for this case?
4. Identify and describe agencies and other services in your community that might be helpful to parents of children with attentional disorders.

Esther Freed watched from the other side of the classroom as Sam cajoled his full-time aide into writing his responses to the social studies questions. This scene seemed to be happening over and over in one form or another since Sam had been diagnosed with Tourette's syndrome three weeks earlier and an aide had been assigned to him. Esther felt that Sam was capable of doing his writing himself.

SCHOOL AND COMMUNITY

Summit Elementary School was located in Lakeside, a thriving upper-middle-class suburban community. The building had been recently remodeled and accommodated kindergarten through fourth grade, with two classes for each grade.

The school benefited from its location at the center of Lakeside. Everything in this well-kept town was within walking distance—the police station, the fire station, the supermarket, and a variety of other stores and offices. Citizens identified with their outstanding school system and took pride when the school used the community as a resource. Children regularly made field trips to places like the veterinarian's office or the supermarket as part of their studies.

Esther Freed had been teaching for five years. Her colleagues considered her energetic, highly competent, caring, and creative in her work with children. She had a reputation for being able to handle anything. Parents often requested her to be their child's teacher.

Esther particularly enjoyed teaching fourth grade. She believed that by this age children had become more independent and were capable of using their basic skills to study a wide range of intriguing subjects and topics. They were also ready to study a topic in some depth. For example, this year the children were studying the solar system: reading books about it, writing their own books about the various planets, constructing mobiles and scale models.

Esther was delighted to see the children so enthusiastically involved in their studies. She often moved among the children as they worked on their projects, giving suggestions, prodding those who needed to be sparked, and generally cheering them on. Her energy seemed to radiate throughout the room.

THE CHILD AND FAMILY

Sam Weiss, a nine-year-old, was the youngest child of Sarah and John Weiss. Mr. Weiss was a successful businessman. Mrs. Weiss had been a full-time mother for many years. In June, she had finished training as a dental hygienist. Mr. and Mrs. Weiss also had a 16-year-old son and a 14-year-old daughter. Sam's brother and sister had been delighted when their baby brother was born and doted on him.

After his first few weeks of school in September, Sam had missed a month for health reasons. During that time, he was diagnosed with Tourette's syndrome and began to receive medical treatment.

The week before Sam returned to school, the Planning and Placement Team (PPT) met to develop an individualized education program for him, as required by law. The principal, the special education teacher, the school nurse, Esther Freed, and Mr. and Mrs. Weiss attended the meeting. The Weisses had brought the reports from the medical assessment and shared information about Tourette's syndrome with the group.

They explained that Tourette's syndrome is an inherited neurological disorder characterized by involuntary motor and vocal tics. A child with Tourette's syndrome may suddenly twitch his head, shoulders, or body, or blink or roll his eyes. Sometimes children tap or drum or touch things repeatedly. The involuntary vocal tics include uttering noises or words. The child may cough, clear his throat, laugh, or yell unexpectedly. Many children with Tourette's syndrome also have attention problems and learning disabilities. Because of problems with visual-motor integration, written work is often hard for them.

However, the school nurse added, there is no "typical" child with Tourette's syndrome. Like all children, they vary in terms of intelligence and other abilities. Moreover, the severity of the symptoms may wax and wane, and the symptoms may change over time.

Mr. and Mrs. Weiss still seemed to be reeling from the diagnosis. They weren't sure how Sam's and their lives would be affected. Mrs. Weiss had just landed her first job as a dental hygienist and was debating whether it was a good time to take on new responsibilities. They didn't know of anyone else in their families who had Tourette's syndrome and so had no warning. They were distressed that Sam had inherited this and seemed to feel guilty about somehow "giving" it to him.

One thing they knew for sure—their child would get the best services possible. They requested that the school assign a full-time aide to Sam and, based on the medical reports, the nurse and special education teacher agreed that this was wise. Never having worked with a child with Tourette's sndrome, Esther did not question this. Sam would also have therapeutic physical education classes with the physical education teacher twice a week.

After the PPT meeting, the special education teacher, Cindy Fieldstone, grabbed Esther for a couple of minutes. She assured Esther that she would be available to consult with her and to answer any questions. Cindy was responsible for many children with special needs, and Esther hoped that Cindy would have time to meet with her periodically.

SAM RETURNS TO SCHOOL

Esther had tried to make Sam's return to school as easy as possible. With the Weiss' encouragement, she had talked to the other children about some of the symptoms of Sam's illness. She asked them to treat Sam normally and help him to feel comfortable.

Sam was a well-mannered, agreeable child. A science buff, he loved to go to natural history museums and had an extensive insect collection. Esther looked forward to his contributions to the solar system unit.

However, she had observed during the first few weeks of school before his absence that Sam tended to tune out at times. She thought this occurred when he wasn't as interested in a subject or task. One time, when the children were supposed to be practicing their times table, Sam sat leafing through a book on ant colonies.

In the two weeks that Sam had been back at school, Esther felt that he was becoming even less attentive. She often noticed him sitting in his chair with a glazed look on his face. Sometimes he doodled rather than completing an assignment. When she would go over to him to remind him to get to work, he would turn to Maria Esposito, his aide, and say, "You write this for me. My hands are shaking too much and I can't hold a pencil."

This was Esther's first experience working with an aide. She knew the background and training of aides could vary widely. Some had special education degrees but had been unable to get full-time teaching positions. Others did not have formal training but had learned a great deal from years of experience, and some were pure beginners.

Maria seemed brand new to this sort of work, and unfortunately, Esther never had much time to talk with her. Maria's hours coincided exactly with Sam's because the school system had not been willing to fund any extra time. Also, Esther never seemed to have an extra moment during the course of the day. She was kept extremely busy by her lively group of 26 fourth graders.

THE SITUATION DETERIORATES

Esther was sympathetic to the many changes in Sam's life and the adjustment that he and his family were making. She knew, too, that he was taking medication that might be affecting him. Still, she began to wonder whether he was intentionally manipulating the situation to avoid his work. Although she had observed that Sam's face occasionally twitched and he sometimes made grunting sounds, she had never noticed his hands shaking.

During the next few days, she conscientiously observed him at regular intervals throughout the school day to check systematically for hand shaking. She never saw Sam's hand shaking at all, yet Maria was doing most of his writing. She remembered that Mrs. Weiss had told her that some children with Tourette's syndrome were able to control their symptoms for seconds or even longer periods. But, she wondered, could Sam suppress his tics for an entire school day?

One time, near the end of the day, Esther asked Sam, "Why aren't you doing your writing yourself?" "My mom told me that if I can't do something, Maria will do it for me," he replied. "I know Maria is here to help you, but it's important for you to try to do as much of your own work as possible," Esther responded with an encouraging tone. "You'll learn more that way."

Then Esther took Maria aside. First, she apologized to Maria for having had so little time to confer with her. Next, she emphasized that Maria needed to let Sam do his own writing. As Maria was nodding in agreement, Esther received a call from the office on her loudspeaker and had to respond to it. Although she hadn't had a chance to get back to Maria, Esther went home at the end of the day feeling like she was making some progress. But, the next morning, she observed Maria again writing for Sam.

Although Sam continued to claim that he could not write because of his illness, he participated eagerly in the construction of the model of the solar system and other activities. He seemed to have no trouble molding the papier-maché or writing labels for the planets. He also engaged readily in other activities he seemed to enjoy.

One day, Esther asked the children to write their fifteen spelling words two times each. Sam turned to his aide and asked her to do the work. Quickly, Esther decided to intervene. She walked over to Sam and asked if his hands were shaking. Somewhat testily, he replied that his mother had told him that the aide would do his writing. "The aide is here to help you," Esther said, "she's not here to take over your work. You need to complete your own assignments." She said it quietly, but firmly.

Sam, who was generally even-tempered, stunned Esther by his reaction. His face flushed and he shouted angrily, "I'm going to listen to my mother, not to you. If you make me write these words, I'm going to tell my mother!"

Discussion Questions

1. What immediate problem(s) is Esther facing? What are the underlying issues?
   - Do you think it is possible that Sam might be suppressing the shaking all day?
   - Could Esther have documented Sam's writing capability? If so, what kinds of activities could be arranged for Sam to participate in?
   - Is a full-time aide warranted for a child with Sam's degree of disability? Consider the allocation of resources in a school system.
2. How might the problem(s) have been avoided?
   - Consider the feasibility of training for Maria and Esther.
   - Evaluate Esther's communication with the Weisses.
   - Should any other members of the school staff be more involved? Who and why?
3. What might the Weisses feel about their son's Tourette's syndrome?
4. What questions do you have about the case that have not been answered?
5. What should Esther do now?

Suggested Activities

1. Role-play a conference between Esther and the Weisses during which Esther questions the appropriate responsibilities for the aide. Work in trios and alternate the role of teacher and parents. What might be the concerns of each? Which are similar and which are different?
2. Identify and gather information from agencies in your community that assist parents who have children with special needs. What guidelines, if any, do they suggest for parent-teacher partnerships to help the child in the classroom?
3. Interview someone who works as a classroom aide to a child with special needs. How have this aide's responsibilities been defined? What difficulties, if any, has the aide encountered in working with the classroom teacher, the child, or the child's parents?
4. Write a research paper on possible causes, symptoms, and treatments for Tourette's syndrome. What strategies are recommended for helping a student with Tourette's syndrome in the classroom? Based on your research, what are your thoughts on Sam's behavior?

Special Education

CHARACTERS

Principal:	Robert Hughes
Special education teacher:	Lois Cohen
Sixth-grade science teacher:	Nancy Evans
Sixth grade-reading teacher:	Arnold Evertson
Guidance counselor:	Daniel Bickford
Special education coordinator:	Amy Fredericks
Student:	Adam Grodsky
Parent:	Helen Grodsky

Mrs. Grodsky was poring over the financial records from the family business, trying to assess whether it was finally coming out of the hole after her husband's sudden death a year and a half before. It was the first day of school, a hot afternoon on an early September day. Her three children had gone off cheerily this morning, eager at least to see their friends, if not to settle down to some hard work. Stephanie and Steve were in high school and were doing well. Adam, a sixth grader, was another story. She hoped he would pull himself out of his slump this year.

She heard the kitchen door slam, and Adam burst into the room. One glance at his flushed face told her that it was not the September heat that had reddened it.

"Mom, how could you let them do this? Why didn't you tell me?" shouted Adam.

"Tell you what?" Helen Grodsky asked. "Calm down, honey, and tell me what's wrong." Adam's lower lip was trembling; he seemed on the verge of tears. Four and a half feet tall and thin, Adam looked younger than his 12 years.

"You didn't know they were going to put me in with those . . . those . . . special ed kids? Mom, some of them can't even read! And I didn't see any of my friends all day! Mr. Hughes just grabbed me in the hall first thing this morning, took me down to Mrs. Cohen's room, and told me this would be my class this year. I'm *not* goin' back there!"

Mrs. Grodsky was stunned and appalled. "Adam, believe me, I didn't know about this myself. Last May, when I met with your teachers and Mr. Hughes, we talked about the problems you were having. All they said was that you needed a 'special program.' Nobody said anything about a special education class. I don't understand. . . ." She paused before continuing and searched her son's distraught face. "Let me call Mr. Hughes and find out what this is about. It must be a mistake."

Adam stalked to his room, slammed the door, and put on a loud tape. She wondered if that was to muffle the sound of sobs. Helen Grodsky made a cup of tea and tried to calm herself. She knew that Mrs. Cohen's class was for students who were emotionally disturbed and learning disabled. There must have been a mix-up!

The summer had gone so smoothly. She had not expected there would be problems on Adam's first day back to school. On the other hand, so much that was unexpected had happened in the last year and a half.

THE SCHOOL AND COMMUNITY

Adam attended Killingham Elementary School in the town of Claymont. A small town of about 12,000, Claymont was in the valley of the Pequot River, which had once provided power for many factories. As the older industries declined, the town's overall economy had floundered.

Claymont's residents were primarily blue collar and working class. They worked in the few small factories that remained or in local businesses. After graduating from high school or college, young people often left the town in search of greater opportunity. They tended, however, to maintain their sense of identity as "Valley" people.

The schools, too, had suffered from the area's slumping economy. As the tax base diminished, funding for the schools was cut. The educational system appeared stuck in the 1970s, and few new teachers were hired. Many of the older teachers seemed simply to be biding their time until retirement.

Killingham Elementary School had been built in 1950 when the town was thriving and its population was growing. Now the facade of the one-story brick building was dirty and weather-beaten. The entry had faded to a grayish-blue and was decorated with tattered posters that looked like vestiges of a previous generation. The classrooms were hardly more appealing.

Mr. Hughes had taught for several years before he became a principal. Killingham was the third school he had headed, and he intended it to be his last. In two years, he planned to retire and move south. Although he occasionally read about new trends in education, he approached issues in a traditional manner. A formidable figure, he believed that it was important for a principal to define clearly the educational mission of the school for the teachers and to act as a strong disciplinarian with the students.

Killingham had about 350 students in its kindergarten through sixth grades. In the fifth and sixth grades, students changed classes for a few of their subjects, to get them ready for their move to the junior high school. Most of the students enjoyed this and viewed it as a sign that they were growing up.

THE STUDENT AND FAMILY

The Grodsky family had lived in Claymont for generations. Both Helen and Paul Grodsky had grown up there and had been high school sweethearts. They married shortly after graduating from the local community college. Then Paul opened his own service station. He developed a reputation as an able mechanic and an honest businessman, and the garage became a modest success.

Once Adam started school, Helen worked side by side with her husband. She booked appointments, answered the telephone, and was responsible for the accounting. Sometimes, after school or during vacations, the children would help out too. Steven was quite handy with tools, and his father began to teach him his trade.

A large burly man, Paul was warm and affectionate. He carved out time from the business to coach his kids' sports teams and to attend important school events. While not bookish himself, he was extremely proud that his two older children, high school students, were on the honor roll and that Adam, too, was such a capable student.

Then, unexpectedly, at the age of 46, Paul died of a massive heart attack. His death threw the family into a tailspin. Stephanie and Steve seemed as devastated as their mother. Everyone was surprised that Adam, the youngest and closest to Paul, appeared to be managing so well. He continued to get As and Bs in fourth grade and took on the role of trying to cheer up the other members of his family.

FIFTH GRADE PROBLEMS

The problems began when Adam started fifth grade. There were continual battles at home. He argued relentlessly with his mother and, with the slightest provocation, shouted at his brother and sister with whom he had once been so close. When he wasn't fighting, he was sullen and silent or retreated to his room for long periods.

The school began to call home. Nancy Evans, the science teacher, contacted Helen to let her know that Adam wasn't handing in his homework. He had been an outstanding science student, and she hoped he wouldn't let things slide. The guidance counselor, Daniel Bickford, called to tell her that several teachers had reported that Adam was disrupting classes and often skipping them. He seemed to have lost his motivation and was unresponsive to either encouragement or reprimands from teachers.

Helen's heart went out to her son. She realized that he was finally beginning to express his grief, and she hoped that even if he vented his anger at home, he would continue to manage well at school. Now it was obvious that he couldn't.

She was barely coping herself. She still missed her husband every day and longed to have his cheerful, comforting presence by her side. She had been confronted right away with the need to attend to the business and to care for her three children. She had hired another mechanic, but the business was just scraping by.

Helen recognized that she could not handle Adam's delayed grief reaction alone. She consulted with her parish priest, and he recommended that she call a family service agency about counseling for Adam. Helen arranged for Adam to receive counseling once a week from a social worker. These sessions helped Adam and he became less belligerent at home. However, he continued to have difficulties at school.

An Upsetting Incident at the End of Fifth Grade

Adam got along well with only one of his fifth-grade teachers, Mrs. Evans, the science teacher. He was apathetic toward the others but expressed real animosity toward Mr. Evertson, the reading teacher. Mr. Evertson had been teaching for over 30 years. He often complained in the teacher's room about the decline in students' behavior over the years. He realized that he had become less patient, especially in the past two years since his back pain had increased. Still, he believed schools let students get away with too much these days.

One day in early May, Adam had been sitting in his reading and language arts class. His eyes wandered toward the window and he watched the birds flitting across the lawn. His reverie was interrupted by Mr. Evertson's voice.

"Adam, what's the matter with you? Why aren't you paying attention?" He walked across the room and laid his hand on Adam's shoulder. "You've got to change your attitude and focus more."

Adam stared straight ahead. "Please take your hand off me," he said calmly and deliberately.

Mr. Evertson proceeded to put his arm around Adam's shoulders. "Now, Adam, you know I want what's best for you. . . ."

Adam jerked away and stood up. "I said, take your hand off me before I kill you!"

Mr. Evertson walked away and called the office on his intercom. At the end of the school day, he went directly to the police station to file a report stating that Adam Grodsky had threatened his life.

The next day, Helen received a call from the principal, Robert Hughes. He said that Adam had threatened a teacher; moreover, he was in danger of failing fifth grade and might have to repeat it. It was crucial that they meet, and soon. Helen agreed to an appointment for the next day.

Helen was distraught. She knew there had been problems, but she couldn't imagine that Adam needed to be retained. She immediately contacted Adam's social worker and asked for her evaluation of the situation. The social worker was equally dismayed and assured Helen that such extreme action was not warranted. She would write a report for Helen to take to the meeting.

THE CONFERENCE

The next day, Helen left the business in the hands of her mechanic and rushed to pick up the social worker's report. Upon arriving at school, the principal ushered her into a conference room. The entire fifth-grade teaching staff, the school psychologist, the special education coordinator and her assistant, and the guidance counselor were seated around the oblong table. Mr. Hughes positioned Helen at one end of the long table and then sat down at the opposite end.

After the teachers had expressed their concerns about Adam, Helen read them the social worker's report. It stated clearly that Adam's problems were related to his father's death. Since they were of an emotional, not an academic, nature, retaining Adam would in all likelihood be damaging to his self-esteem. Moreover, in light of his difficult relations with his reading teacher, he should not repeat that class.

After she was finished reading, there was a brief silence. Then Amy Frederick, the special education coordinator, responded. "Well, we'll just have to plan a special program for him. If you have any further questions, we're always available to meet with you." Then she asked Helen to sign a form.

Helen went home that day feeling that things had been resolved. She felt that the social worker's report had been convincing, and that the staff was now ready to make some accommodations to the trauma that Adam had experienced and the behavior that it had produced. Reflecting upon this meeting later, Helen commented, "I was so relieved that the staff had dropped the idea of retaining Adam that I didn't question what they meant by a 'special' program. The form was confusing, but I just skimmed it, signed it, and got out of there quickly before they could change their minds."

During the summer, Adam was much calmer. His baseball team had had a good season, and he seemed to feel proud of his role as catcher. He got along reasonably well with his teammates, other friends, and family. He even seemed to be looking forward to sixth grade.

THE FIRST DAY OF SIXTH GRADE

Drinking her tea and trying to compose herself after Adam's outburst, Helen thought about what to do. How could Adam have been placed in a special education class? She never agreed to that. Was it possible that the school had been right? Was he, in fact, violent? She longed to turn to Paul for reassuring advice. Then she remembered the turtles.

In early July, Adam and his friend John had been walking through the woods when they stumbled upon a nest of eggs. The boys brought them back to Adam's house and hunted through Adam's extensive library on wildlife and the natural world to try to figure out what kind of eggs they were. After determining that they were turtle eggs, Adam painstakingly constructed an incubator, using concepts that he had learned in science during fifth grade. He lovingly tended to the eggs and when the turtles hatched, he released them in a local state park.

No, Helen thought to herself, this was not a violent child. She knew she had to fight the school's decision to place Adam in a special education class. She telephoned Mr. Hughes and made an appointment to speak with him that afternoon.

THE MEETING

The meeting was held in the same room where last spring's conference was held. This time, only Mr. Hughes and Mrs. Fredericks were present. Helen had hoped Mr. Bickford, the guidance counselor, would be there as well. Most of her previous conversations about Adam had been with him, and he seemed understanding of the difficulties Adam had faced. She asked where Mr. Bickford was, but Mr. Hughes explained that he had had another meeting at this time.

When Helen expressed her distress over Adam's placement, Mrs. Fredericks responded, "But you agreed to the special program back in May when you signed the form!"

Helen was outraged. "But you didn't tell me that it meant a special education classroom! I almost had to file for bankruptcy that month! You expect me to read minds, too?"

Mr. Hughes and Mrs. Fredericks were sympathetic but tried to convince Helen that Adam would do better in Mrs. Cohen's class. It was completely self-contained, so his friends would not be present to distract him. Moreover, it would give him a chance to get extra tutoring in the academic areas. He had failed reading, and his other grades were low, too. If he showed significant improvement, he could always be moved back to regular classes. Finally, it was important not to forget the concern about his emotional development. After all, he had threatened a teacher's life.

Discussion Questions

1. What do you see as the problem(s) in this case?
2. How did this situation develop?

- How might Adam's personal life have affected his school performance?
- How might school factors have affected Adam's behavior?
3. How would you evaluate the school personnel's actions?
4. What are the legal issues in this case?
5. If you were Helen Grodsky, what would you do at this point?
6. If you were the school personnel, what would you do?
   - What might be the long-term consequences if Adam stays in the special education class? Consider possible advantages and disadvantages.
7. How would you compare the effect of Mr. Grodsky's death on Adam's school performance to the effect that a divorce might have on a child? What might be the similarities? Differences?

Suggested Activities

1. Role-play both conferences that Helen Grodsky has with school personnel. Alternate roles so that you can examine issues from differing perspectives. Consider other strategies that might have changed the style and outcome of the conferences.
2. Review the literature on the effect of a personal loss, through death or divorce, on children's school performance and write a report on your findings.
3. Interview a school psychologist or school social worker who has worked with children who have experienced death or divorce in their families. What strategies has she or he used to help students cope with their experiences? What programs, if any, does the school have to help children facing such losses? How have teachers been involved? How have parents been involved?

Support or Threat?

Outreach parent counselor: Lynn Evans
Parents: Pam and John Jamison

Lynn Evans, an outreach parent counselor, had started visiting the Jamisons' home only two weeks ago. She was just beginning to feel as if she were making some headway in helping Pam Jamison to gain control over her life. She rang the bell on Tuesday morning, expecting Pam to answer. Instead, Pam's husband, John, opened the door. "Oh, no," thought Lynn. She couldn't believe that Pam had allowed her husband to move back in—not after he had abused their daughter.

THE PARENT AIDE PROGRAM

The parent aide program was a service of the child guidance clinic in Hamilton, a city of 95,000. The program was designed to assist parents who were under stress or whose children were at risk of neglect or abuse. Some of the clients were teen parents or first-time parents who didn't have their own parents or other adults in their area from whom they could get help or counsel. Others had mental health or domestic violence problems. There were parents who had been homeless, had a family member with a disability, or were contending with other special problems. Referrals of families came from various sources: substance abuse prevention programs, the hospital, or the Department of Children and Families.

The parent aide program was a free and voluntary home visiting program. The aide typically visited a family once or twice a week for ninety minutes at the parent's request. Parents chose the number of visits they preferred and the areas they wanted help with. As the needs of the family changed, the services could change as well.

Aides generally advised parents in areas such as child guidance, household management, and nutrition. They tried to build a parent's confidence and self-esteem, teach effective discipline methods, and improve parent-child communication. Aides often acted as sounding boards, role models, and counselors. As one aide commented, "A lot of times, we're the first ones who have listened to parents' problems."

THE PARENT AIDE

Lynn Evans had an undergraduate degree in special education and experience as a day-care teacher, substitute teacher, and home tutor. She had decided to look for part-time work so that she could continue to spend half the day with her three young children. One day while looking through the paper she chanced upon a listing for a parent aide.

She was comfortable with the idea of visiting homes because of her work as a home tutor. She knew how hard it was to be a parent. During the interview process, she acknowledged, "I know I will see a lot of things that will surprise and shock me, but my role is to stay open-minded so I can help."

For training, Lynn was sent to a series of workshops and seminars. She met weekly with a supportive, knowledgeable supervisor to discuss the families with whom she had begun to work. Many parents, she learned, had never developed the skills to deal with the stresses of parenting and daily life. "You have to take them where they're at and work with them," she commented. Sometimes, this was as simple as teaching some nursery rhymes to a mother who wanted to sing to her child. Often, it was more complicated.

THE FAMILY

Pam Jamison was 25 years old. Her first two children, a six-year-old girl and an eight-year-old boy, were from her first marriage. Her third child, a five-month-old girl, was from her marriage with John Jamison.

Pam's first marriage had ended in divorce. She had dropped out of high school to marry Bill, a traveling salesman. Frequently away from home, he eventually just left for good. "We had two kids and it got a little tough, so he just took off," she said. She was bitter that he had taken what little savings they had, and she was left to raise the children on a shoestring.

While growing up, she had watched several members of her family struggle with alcoholism. Despite the strife in her relationships with her brothers and sisters, they remained very much involved with each other. Moreover, her parents' and her siblings' marriages had stayed together, even though there were many problems. Pam's ideal of an enduring marriage had been shattered when Bill left her.

When Lynn first visited Pam, her six-year-old was recovering from burns on her back. At the hospital, Pam had told the doctor that it was an accident. However, the doctor suspected child abuse and reported the family to the

Department of Youth and Families. The department investigated but did not find evidence of child abuse in the family. Nevertheless, the outreach worker was concerned that Pam seemed very depressed and neither the house nor the children were well cared for. She made a referral to the parent aide program so that Pam would have some support.

THE FIRST FEW VISITS

On Lynn's first visit, Pam answered the doorbell holding the baby, whose diaper reeked of urine. Lynn was appalled by the flies swarming in the kitchen and the mounds of garbage in the house but was determined not to show her feelings. She gingerly began to establish some rapport with Pam. As they talked, she learned that Mr. Jamison had recently moved out of the house.

Lynn's second visit was in the late afternoon. The older children were just arriving home from school. Sam, eight, dropped his lunch box on the floor and ran to get a snack. He slipped on the Cheerios that littered the floor and spilled some milk when he tried to pour himself a glass. Pam shouted at Sam to be more careful. The children went upstairs with their snacks and played for a long time unattended.

Pam expected the children to take care of themselves. They had to cross a busy street and walk to the bus stop alone in the morning—often without their socks, jackets, or lunches. The laundry was strewn all over the living room, yet Pam expected the children to find clean underwear in the morning. Pam mentioned once how angry she'd been at Sam when, as a four-year-old, he'd run outside and down the street. Her comments to her children were mostly negative. "Don't be so lazy!" or "You're a slow poke!" she'd call to them.

Lynn was particularly shocked to find that the children had no toothbrushes. Pam seemed to have no sense that this was even a problem. Lynn knew she could not show her distress but wondered how she could begin to make Pam more aware of her children's health and emotional needs.

She began to work with Pam in small ways. Lynn suggested what reasonable expectations for young children might be. They discussed the need for safety locks and toothbrushes, for example. But Pam had many excuses. When the dinner dishes were still piled in the sink one midmorning, she grumbled, "I was tired at the end of the night and couldn't wash them." Lynn tried to be firm but supportive. "They *have* to be done. What's the best time for you? How can you pace yourself?" This time, Lynn offered to wash the dishes with her, and they talked as they worked.

Lynn knew that the family would be a challenge. Pam had mentioned on her first visit that she had agreed to home visits before but had stopped them. Although Pam didn't explain why, Lynn was aware that families stopped services for various reasons. Sometimes the parent aide was unable to establish good rapport; other times there were circumstances in the family, such as depression or drug abuse, that lead families to stop participating.

Lynn wanted the parent aide program to work this time. She had heard other home visitors making degrading comments about families, criticizing people for being on welfare or assuming that they didn't have much of an education. She was appalled when she heard them speak condescendingly to parents.

Although she was still new to this work, she realized that she had to find ways to help Pam understand young children and their needs—without offending her. First she had to gain Pam's trust, or Pam might drop out of the program again. Then she had to help Pam in such a way that Pam could begin to help herself, without being overly dependent on Lynn. The ultimate goal was for Pam to take care of her children properly.

So far, she seemed to be developing a positive relationship with Pam. Just the fact that Pam was home when she arrived was a good sign.

FATHER RETURNS HOME

Two weeks after Lynn had started visiting the Jamison family, John Jamison returned home to live. Lynn was stunned that Pam would allow him to come back. Although Lynn didn't know for sure, she strongly suspected that Mr. Jamison had purposely burned his daughter. Pam didn't raise this possibility and simply commented about her husband to Lynn, "Yeah, he gets a little rough with the kids." Lynn had tried to subtly question the little girl about the burns, but she just said, "Daddy gets real angry." He seemed to have such control over the family.

Although Pam's extended family was opposed to his return, Pam felt that was because everyone was against him. "My family doesn't see how he's changed," she complained to Lynn. "We were together over the weekend and even though the kids were tough, he was fine. Everything was fine."

But Lynn viewed the situation differently and felt that Pam was putting her children at risk. She saw John as a ticking time bomb. Pam had told her that he himself had been abused as a child.

Pam sometimes read the advice columns in the newspapers on various physical and mental health issues. She once mused that John might have an attention-deficit disorder and thought vitamins would help him to control his temper. "He's been taking his vitamin B. He's doing good," she commented to Lynn.

When Lynn first met John, she thought to herself, "What a smooth talker!" Once when she was there he greeted the children in a friendly way after school and politely reminded them to hang up their jackets and put away their lunch boxes—as if this were their daily routine. He never admitted to any frustration or problems with the children. He acted confident but rarely looked Lynn in the eye. His face had a masklike expression. "Oh, the baby's wet. I'd better go change her," he'd say in a saccharine tone. But Lynn knew that this wasn't typical; she'd seen the baby's diaper rash.

Without angering him, she needed to help him to develop some appropriate strategies for dealing with the children and managing his own rage.

She was careful never to criticize him directly. She would talk sympathetically about how stressful parenting young children could be. In a low-key way, she suggested some videos on disciplining children that other parents had found informative. A week later, she gave him a list of 12 alternatives to spanking. She thought these simple strategies, such as counting to 10 or shouting into a pillow, might help him. She wasn't confident that he could read, so she offered to go over the list with him, but he didn't seem interested.

Lynn worried that if she made a wrong move, she could set him off. Then, after she left, he might blow up and abuse his wife or children. She was walking a fine line.

And she was always worried about leaving the house with the children there. At the end of the last visit, the eight-year-old, Sam, clung to her. Looking up to her with sad, empty eyes, he pleaded, "Take me with you."

Discussion Questions

1. What problem(s) does Lynn face? Which are immediate and which are long-term?
2. What are some factors that may have contributed to this situation?
   - What are some common causes of child abuse and neglect in a family? Are any of these present in this situation?
   - Describe Pam, including her needs, personality, and background. How might she be contributing to the problem?
   - Describe John Jamison.
   - What might be the effect of Lynn's newness to the job?
3. Describe how Lynn, Pam, John, and the children might perceive this situation.
   - Why might Pam refuse to acknowledge that there is possible abuse?
4. What should Lynn do now?
   - How can she build a trusting relationship with Pam?
   - How can she teach John some strategies to manage his anger and interact better with the children?
   - Should she remove the children? Does she have the power to do so? If she does, what other risks are there?
5. Should Lynn call on other sources of support for the family? If so, what might these be?
6. How do the issues in this case relate to issues you might face in a school-based situation?

Suggested Activities

1. Role-play a meeting between Lynn and Pam at which Lynn tries to help Pam face some of her problems, and consider some ways to respond.

2. Role-play a meeting between Lynn, Pam, and John Jamison. What are the concerns of each? How might these be addressed?
3. Interview a professional, such as a special educator or a social worker, who has worked with children who have been abused. What kinds of needs have they seen in the children and how have they attempted to address these?
4. Review research on child abuse and neglect. Write a paper that identifies contributing factors and strategies to deal with this problem. What problems do professionals face finding conclusive evidence for abuse?

Six members of the Planning and Placement Team (PPT) were arrayed around the table, waiting expectantly for Mrs. Hendrick to get to her point. They had rushed from their various commitments to get to the meeting on time. The principal, speech-language pathologist, director of pupil personnel services, occupational therapist, special educator, and aide were present at Mrs. Hendrick's request, presumably to discuss an urgent issue relating to her son, Alan. Alan, a first grader, was in Joe Shea's special education classroom.

Joe couldn't believe his ears. Mrs. Hendrick had been talking for 10 minutes, and so far she hadn't even mentioned Alan. Instead, she was complaining bitterly that some of the children's lunches were subsidized. She didn't see why she, as a taxpayer, should have to underwrite other children's food costs. Why couldn't those parents fulfill their proper responsibilities? This complaint seemed to be Mrs. Hendrick's sole reason for convening the entire team. Her demands were really getting out of hand.

THE SCHOOL AND COMMUNITY

Sleepy Hollow Elementary School was located in the rural community of Dunham. Although there were still some family-owned farms, the town had become a pastoral retreat for professionals, most of whom worked elsewhere. Some held jobs in the state's capital about twenty miles away. Others taught or worked at a small liberal arts university nearby.

Sleepy Hollow School had about 350 children in its kindergarten through second grades. For many years, there had been little ethnic or racial diversity in the school, however the number of children needing to be taught English as a second language was slowly increasing. Its special services included the recently hired teacher of English as a second language, a special education resource room teacher, two other special education teachers, a social worker, and a part-time school psychologist. In addition, a speech-language pathologist, an occupational therapist, and a physical therapist worked with individual children as needed.

Joe felt that the ambiance of the Sleepy Hollow School was unusually cohesive. Most of the teachers had taught together for several years and enjoyed working together. They shared ideas and supported one another. For every teacher's birthday, there was a special celebration. Joe realized that it might be hard for a newcomer to break into this tight group, although the staff welcomed new teachers and he had never seen them exclude anybody.

The school encouraged family involvement. The principal had an open-door policy, and parents were invited to drop in and share ideas or concerns with her. There were always parents in the building—carrying out projects with children in classes, xeroxing materials for teachers, working in the library, tutoring, and assisting in the art classes. Joe felt their contribution was heartfelt and substantial. There was occasional gossiping and even back-stabbing among the parents, but they knew not to involve the teachers.

Joe taught children who were more severely disabled. He had a self-contained special education classroom for children from kindergarten through second grade. This year, his class included two children who were mentally retarded (one was not toilet trained), two children with language disabilities, one child with social-emotional difficulties, and Alan. For the most part, Joe worked with the children in his classroom. Whenever possible, they were mainstreamed into regular classes and he would then co-teach with the regular teacher.

A tall, friendly man, Joe had been teaching for ten years. His wife was a teacher as well; they had two children. Before coming to Sleepy Hollow five years earlier, Joe had directed a resource room at a high school. He had always been a special education teacher. "It's challenging," he said. "It's not a question of just opening the teacher's manual and repeating a lesson. You never have the same situation twice, so you have to be very creative."

THE CHILD AND FAMILY

Alan Hendrick was the only child of Martha and Robert Hendrick. Both college-educated, Robert was a lawyer and Martha was a real estate agent. Alan was born when Martha was 36 and Robert was 38. They had eagerly anticipated his birth, knowing he would be their only child.

From the moment he was born, Alan was a remarkably beautiful child. Mrs. Hendrick took great pleasure in buying him expensive baby clothes and decking him out for walks in the neighborhood. Both parents were pleased to have a son, hoping he would continue the long line of lawyers in the family.

Although Alan looked like any adorable baby, the Hendricks soon realized that something was not right. By the end of his first year, it was determined that he had a brain disorder. Alan didn't like to be touched and was not developing language. His developmental milestones, such as learning to sit, were delayed. He engaged in self-stimulating behaviors, like rocking.

Mrs. Hendrick had the primary responsibility of caring for their son. Because Mr. Hendrick's law practice required him to go away on frequent business trips, he was rarely involved in the daily care or decision making for Alan.

KINDERGARTEN

Alan started Sleepy Hollow School in a self-contained special education kindergarten class. The occupational therapist worked with him for one hour a week to develop his small motor coordination. The speech-language pathologist also worked one hour a week with him. Although his articulation was clear, Alan hesitated when he spoke, struggling to find words. Joe was not his teacher, but the other special education teacher conferred with him about Alan and his family and asked for Joe's suggestions.

As Alan grew older, his disability became more apparent both to his parents and to others. As Joe remarked, "It's common for parents to become more aware and distressed. It's one thing when their child *is* a baby and his behavior is babyish. But as the child gets older, the inappropriate behavior becomes more noticeable and upsetting."

At home, Alan had become very controlling and aggressive. Sensitive to noise, he shrieked when the radio seemed too loud and Mrs. Hendrick would rush to turn down the volume. He refused to take his medicine, although his mother tried to disguise the taste with honey or peanut butter. He even became dangerous to himself and others. Once he grabbed his mother's hands as she was driving. Another time he hurled a rock at a child on the playground.

Mrs. Hendrick's own moods would swing. Some days she seemed to recognize the severity of Alan's difficulties and would admit to despair. "Get rid of this kid. I can't take him anymore," she once commented to Alan's teacher.

On other days, she asserted that Alan didn't even belong in the special education classroom. "What's he doing in here? He's learning to act this way from the other kids, and you're not teaching him anything anyway. This is just holding him back," she complained bitterly. Still, the school kept Alan in the self-contained classroom.

FIRST GRADE

Alan was placed in Joe's special education classroom for first grade. In the fall, he began to be mainstreamed into regular classes for art, music, and physical education. These were a challenge for him. In physical education, it was hard for him to follow directions. Because of his poor fine motor coordination, art was difficult. He needed an aide with him at times.

Joe worked with Alan in the academic areas. Alan had grown more talkative by this time and was beginning to read. His intelligence was in the low to average range.

Joe taught Alan individually and as part of a small group. Alan seemed unable to focus on a task for more than five or ten minutes. He might be reading and then look up and gaze off into the distance. He might do one simple addition problem but not complete the other two on the page. He would perseverate, singing a song or writing the same words over and over.

At times, Alan was very sweet. He tried to do his best and to please Joe. At other times, he seemed manipulative. He would bump into another child and then accuse that child of bumping into him. He would wait until he had an audience before performing a generous act on the playground, like giving up his swing to someone else. He sometimes complained to his mother about kids teasing him, but Joe saw no evidence of it.

A FORMIDABLE PARENT

By November, Mrs. Hendrick had given up her job and was devoting herself full-time to her son. As Alan grew stronger and more aggressive at home, her manner became more insistent. Every day or two, the staff received a call or visit from Mrs. Hendrick.

In cold weather, she wanted the teachers to be sure that Alan wore his gloves at all times, despite the fact that there might be 150 kids on the playground to supervise and Alan liked to yank them off when no one was looking.

More important, she informed the staff that she didn't want Alan labeled, nor did she want him in the special education classroom. She felt he wasn't being challenged enough, and that his behavior was deteriorating because he was mimicking the behavior of the other children with special needs. (Joe, on the other hand, felt that his behaviors tended to be more inappropriate than the others.) She didn't want him to see the occupational therapist or the speech-language pathologist, because this deprived him of time he could be spending on academics or with normal children. She wanted daily reports from all of the staff who worked with Alan.

Mrs. Hendrick complained about other children being mean to Alan and calling him names. She wanted the teachers to arrange every day for a child to sit next to Alan at lunch or to play with him outdoors. "She just doesn't realize that you can't control other kids that way," Joe commented.

Furthermore, Mrs. Hendrick didn't like the children whom Alan *was* tentatively beginning to make friends with in Joe's classroom. She criticized their parents, saying, "They must have done something wrong to have children like that." She tried to discuss aspects of other parents' lives with the staff.

The staff began to feel harassed by Mrs. Hendrick's telephone calls. She called them at school during the day and at their homes during the evening. Everyone received calls, including the principal, the director of pupil personnel, the school social worker, Joe, the occupational therapist, the speech-language pathologist, the secretaries, and even the cook.

The phone calls could easily last an hour. Joe's strategy was to let her talk, to express everything she was feeling. He listened to her initially because she just might say something that was crucial for him to know about Alan. He would excuse himself if the call went on for too long, stating, "I have to go to playground duty," or "My dinner is on the table."

The secretaries screened her calls to administrators. That didn't stop Mrs. Hendrick, however. She simply came to school to speak to them or the teachers personally.

By midyear, Mrs. Hendrick was coming to school almost daily. She tended to stay for a while in Joe's class, and Alan became distracted and would cling to her. The visits disrupted his learning and that of the other children. Finally, the PPT made a rule that Mrs. Hendrick couldn't enter the classrooms; they would meet with her outside the rooms.

Mrs. Hendrick frequently requested PPT meetings. By law, this was a parent's prerogative, and the team would have to comply. But often Mrs. Hendrick would ramble on and on, never addressing an issue of importance.

Mrs. Hendrick began to experience difficulty in her relations with other parents as well. She lectured them on how to prepare nutritious meals for their children; she accused one father of harshly disciplining his son. Parents felt she was acting superior and began to shun her son and her. The Cub Scout leader decided that he didn't want to have Alan in his pack.

ATTEMPTS TO HELP MRS. HENDRICK

The team members often conferred with each other about how to deal with this situation. They tried a variety of ways to support Mrs. Hendrick in her role as a parent. Leslie Marks, the school social worker, made several home visits to talk with Mrs. Hendrick in the privacy and comfort of her own home. She also counseled Alan and his mother once a week at school. In addition, she suggested a parenting class in the community, which Mrs. Hendrick found helpful.

Leslie had to set limits on Mrs. Hendrick's telephone calls. Leslie was designated as contact person; Mrs. Hendrick was not to call anyone else on the staff. Moreover, she could only call Leslie at a specific time on a specific day each week.

The team realized that Mrs. Hendrick needed additional support at home. Through a special program, they arranged for an aide to make weekly visits to work with Alan at home and model strategies that his mother could try.

The teachers also tried to work with Mrs. Hendrick. She was invited to observe Alan's classes for art, music, and gym until this became too disruptive. Joe invited her to his class at clearly defined times, to read a story, for example, or to have lunch with the children. This allowed her to participate legitimately in her son's experiences, within set boundaries. She was a room mother, too. She brought in treats for holiday parties and contacted other class parents to enlist their help with fund-raising events.

She was encouraged to participate positively in the larger school community as well. She worked on several committees of the Parent-Teacher Organization. Despite these efforts, Mrs. Hendrick seemed to be disaffected from the other parents and continuously complained to the teachers.

By spring, after repeated requests from Mrs. Hendrick, the teachers decided to mainstream Alan into the regular classroom for reading instruction. Joe had four other students mainstreamed in that room, and he worked with all five of the children. Alan needed the most help. Joe had to direct his behavior every step of the way. If he didn't sit right next to him and tell him to take out his pencil or book, Alan would become distracted and gaze off. The other students with special needs seemed to take cues from watching other children, but Alan was unable to do so.

FULL INCLUSION FOR ALAN?

Mrs. Hendrick insisted that she wanted Alan fully included in the regular second grade in the fall. In May, she systematically cornered each professional who had worked with Alan to argue her position.

Joe was unsure what was best for Alan. On the one hand, the child still needed a great deal of help academically. His reading was poor. He had difficulty remembering previously learned words, decoding new words, and comprehending a passage. Moreover, his social skills were weak. He had to be guided through most social situations. On the playground, for example, he would just wander off if a teacher did not engage him in directed play with other children. There were many social situations he simply didn't comprehend. Joe wasn't sure how Alan would fare having a regular classroom as his home base. And Mrs. Hendrick did not even want him to have an aide because she felt that would stigmatize him further.

On the other hand, Mrs. Hendrick was threatening to pull Alan out of all special services if he weren't fully included in the regular classroom for second grade. She might be erratic, but she was not uninformed—she knew her rights as a parent. At least if the staff appeased her by complying with her demands, she would allow Alan to continue to receive some special services. If they didn't keep Mrs. Hendrick happy, would they be sacrificing Alan's needs? Or perhaps they'd be sacrificing his needs if they did give in to her demand. Joe wasn't sure what to recommend at the final PPT on Alan in mid-June.

Discussion Questions

1. What immediate problem(s) is Joe Shea facing?
2. What are some underlying issues in this case?
3. How might this situation appear from the perspectives of Alan, Mrs. Hendrick, Mr. Hendrick, Joe, and Leslie? Consider the expectations of the various persons involved in this case.
4. How effectively do you feel the staff worked with Mrs. Hendrick? What else might they have done?
   - Would your recommendations differ in a school system with fewer resources?
5. How might Mr. Hendrick have been encouraged to be more involved in his son's schooling?
6. Which should carry the greater weight in determining a child's program— the parents' decision about their child or the professionals' judgment about what is best for the child? Why?
7. If you were Joe, what would you recommend at the PPT? Why? Is there a way to accommodate Mrs. Hendrick's wishes without "sacrificing" Alan's needs?

Suggested Activities

1. Role-play a conference between Joe Shea and Mr. and Mrs. Hendrick at which Joe expresses his concerns about fully including Alan in a regular second-grade classroom. Conduct the role-play a second time, reversing the roles of parents and teacher.
2. Review the rights by law of parents of children with special needs. What are the implications of those rights for this case?
3. Identify and describe services in your community that might be helpful to parents of children with severe behavior disorders.

Double Dilemma

Special education teacher:	Mark Reynolds
First-grade teacher:	Loretta Serkin
Students:	John D'Amico
	David D'Amico
Parents:	Rose and Anthony D'Amico

Mark Reynolds, a resource room teacher, was at a Planning and Placement Team (PPT) meeting. The team was considering how to help John D'Amico, a first grader, who was struggling in school. Both John and his twin brother, David, had been tested recently, and the results were mind-boggling. David met the legal criteria to be identified as learning disabled. Ironically, although John was not doing as well as David, John did not meet the law's requirements for special services.

Mark looked sympathetically across the table at Mr. and Mrs. D'Amico. How could he justify providing services to the higher-functioning twin because he met the criteria and not help the lower-functioning twin?

THE SCHOOL, COMMUNITY, AND TEACHER

Hempstead was an upper-middle-class community of about 15,000 that took pride in its colonial heritage, fine schools, beautiful shoreline, and handsome homes. Its residents were more than willing to commute the half-hour into the city for their jobs in order to escape back to this splendid setting at the end of a hard day.

Hempstead had two schools for children in kindergarten through second grade. Little Creek Elementary School had about 300 children, including a preschool early intervention program. The other school, across town, had a self-contained special education classroom for children from both parts of town, in addition to its regular program.

At Little Creek, there were about 20 students in each class. The teachers, mostly veterans, held onto useful time-honored strategies and eagerly tried out new ideas. They taught reading through a whole language approach with some emphasis on phonics, math through manipulatives, and generally included many experiential activities. They worked to make their classrooms developmentally appropriate.

The professional staff included a reading specialist and three Chapter 1 aides. The aides worked in all of the classes, tutoring children individually in the areas of reading, writing, and some math. There was also a half-time social worker. The full-time school psychologist conducted psychological testing at all the elementary schools but did not work directly with the children.

Mark Reynolds, the special education teacher, spent half-time in each of the kindergarten–second-grade schools. He had been teaching in the resource room at Little Creek School for the past nine years. In this district, the resource room teacher traditionally worked with children who were learning disabled.

A tall, stately, middle-aged man with a ready smile, Mark had been teaching for almost thirty years. He had known he wanted to be a teacher since he was a youngster. When he was 12, he lived next door to a child who was blind. Fascinated by how the child was learning, he decided at that point that he wanted to teach.

At college, Mark majored in psychology. At the graduate level, he trained as a teacher of the blind and visually impaired and taught in that area for twenty years. When his program was phased out, he decided to become certified as a special education teacher because he wanted to continue to work with children individually. Mark was well respected in the school system because of his caring attitude, clear thinking, and professional dedication.

THE CHILD AND THE FAMILY

John D'Amico was a tall, slender, brown-haired child. He and his identical twin, David, lived with their parents in a comfortable three-bedroom home with a spacious backyard. Mr. D'Amico, the manager of the local store of a large discount clothing chain, liked carpentry as a hobby and had built the boys a tree house that they loved. Mrs. D'Amico did not work outside of the home. She found that caring for twins was plenty to occupy her time, and she really enjoyed playing with them and watching them grow.

The boys were born prematurely. As they grew older, their mother began to worry that their language development was slow. When she took them to the early intervention program at Little Creek School to be assessed, her suspicions were confirmed. The boys were identified as needing speech and language therapy, which they began as preschoolers.

For kindergarten, the boys were placed in separate classes. "They're delightful, darling boys," said one of their teachers. However, they were very quiet and rarely interacted with other children. "They knew they had speech differences," commented the teacher. For example, they made substitutions, such as "f" for "th," and used pronouns and verbs improperly. Because they were so shy and soft-spoken and made syntactic errors, they were not always intelligible.

Whenever possible, they sought out each other. They played together at recess and sat together at lunchtime. Despite their problems communicating with others, they seemed to use a private language with each other.

The twins continued to have speech and language therapy in kindergarten. Since they had been born prematurely and were young, both the teachers and the speech-language pathologist attributed their difficulties to developmental factors and hoped they would grow out of them with some help.

FIRST GRADE

Because of the school's efforts to respect their individuality and encourage their independence, John and David were again placed in separate classes in first grade. The boys received speech and language therapy, as well as three half-hour individual sessions per week from the reading teacher and daily tutoring from a Chapter 1 aide.

Both John's and David's teachers noticed that each boy was continuing to struggle. They played with other children but still had trouble communicating, and they gravitated toward each other. Moreover, they were having difficulty in beginning reading tasks such as remembering sound-symbol relationships or writing letters.

At the November conferences, the teachers shared their observations with Mr. and Mrs. D'Amico. Tears welled in Mrs. D'Amico's eyes. Both parents were upset, but they seemed confident that the teachers were trying their best. They had had positive experiences with the school system's early intervention program and comfortable working relationships with their boys' teachers so far. Eager to help out, Mr. D'Amico assured the teachers, "We'll keep working with the boys at home."

PLANNING AND PLACEMENT TEAM MEETING

In the late spring, the school's planning and placement team had separate meetings to discuss speech and language services for each boy. Language was still an issue, but now their classroom teachers also expressed strong concerns about the children's progress in the academic areas. They simply weren't keeping pace with the other students in reading and writing. Math was a relative strength, but John had difficulty with word problems and more abstract mathematical concepts.

Mr. and Mrs. D'Amico had noticed problems at home, so they weren't surprised. John, in particular, was beginning to get frustrated over his homework. He was having a harder time than David at school. Although John was quiet and even withdrawn at school, he had begun to lash out angrily at home.

Mr. and Mrs. D'Amico wanted to do whatever was necessary to help their sons. To help them develop self-confidence and make friends, their parents had involved them in soccer, baseball, and Cub Scouts, where academic work was not the focus. But, clearly, their academic needs had to be addressed too. Both the parents and the professionals wondered whether the children might have problems in areas other than language. They all agreed to have the boys tested to determine this.

Then the team had to decide about the boys' placement for the next year. Everyone concurred that John would benefit from repeating first grade. The decision about David wasn't so clear. His speech had improved, and he was interacting more with other children. Although quiet, he was well liked. Furthermore, the academics came to him more easily. Still, there were serious lags, and the team thought it best for him to repeat first grade, too.

When the boys learned the decisions, David was distressed that he wasn't going on to second grade. He seemed to feel he wasn't measuring up and perceived it as a punishment. John seemed less concerned; he knew he was struggling.

THE TESTING

David's evaluation took place at the end of the year at Little Creek School. John was tested during the summer at a reputable child guidance center that offered a more in-depth evaluation for a modest fee. The D'Amicos decided to take advantage of this because their concerns about John were greater.

WHAT THE LAW SAYS

According to the Individuals with Disabilities Education Act (a federal law) and the state's regulations, a child has a learning disability if:

1. the child doesn't achieve at a level commensurate with his age and ability in one or more specific areas when given appropriate learning experiences, or
2. the child demonstrates a severe discrepancy between his achievement and his intellectual ability or potential in those areas, and
3. this discrepancy cannot be due to visual, hearing, or motor handicaps; mental retardation; emotional disturbance; or environmental, cultural, or economic disadvantage.

TEST RESULTS

John's test results revealed that his intelligence was in the low to average range. Because his intelligence and his achievement scores were consistently low, he did not meet the criteria for being learning disabled.

Moreover, John's full scale IQ was above the number needed to classify him as educable mentally retarded (EMR), so he could not receive services under that exceptionality. Although John was still having trouble making himself clear and performing the expected academic tasks, he was performing at a reasonable level considering his IQ.

David's testing indicated that he had greater ability than John. Furthermore, there were enough points between his cognitive and his achievement scores to identify him as learning disabled.

ANOTHER PLANNING AND PLACEMENT TEAM MEETING

Both John and David were now repeating first grade in separate classrooms with new teachers. In October, the PPT again held separate meetings to consider the results of the testing and to plan for each of them. The meetings included the regular education teacher, Mark (the resource room teacher), the school psychologist, the speech-language pathologist, the principal, and Mr. and Mrs. D'Amico. Mark and the school psychologist were responsible for interpreting the test results to the members of the team. David's test results indicated that he was eligible for resource room help, so the real concern was how John's needs would be met.

Loretta Serkin, John's first grade teacher, began the meeting on John. She described John as a polite, personable child. He was enjoyable and had a good sense of humor. But he still had academic problems, in fact, he was falling further and further behind the other children. For example, he had difficulty identifying sight words and following directions. He was cooperative and willing—certainly not a behavior problem. Yet when school work was hard for him, he became distracted and drifted off. He was self-conscious about his speech, which Ms. Serkin saw as a significant cause of his weakness in oral and written language. "He needs to develop confidence," she commented.

The speech-language pathologist added that John's progress had been slow. He had problems using correct syntax, forming negatives, and asking questions. "He needs modeling," she suggested. She then raised the possibility of placing him in the self-contained special education classroom, where the class size would be smaller and the teacher could work more directly with him to model and encourage appropriate language. However, she noted there would be a lack of peer models in this class. The self-contained classroom was located in the kindergarten–second-grade school on the other side of town, so John would have to take the bus there. It served many children with language problems, as well as children with other disabilities.

Mr. and Mrs. D'Amico balked at the idea of having the twins in two different schools. They felt that John was already starting to feel badly about himself and that sending him to another school would accentuate these feelings. At least, so far this year, he seemed a little happier than he had last year. The emotional toll of moving him would be greater than the emotional toll of letting him struggle academically for another year.

At this point, the principal jumped in. "Well, if we're talking about placing John in a self-contained special education classroom because of the severity of his language problems, why can't we consider giving him resource room help right here in the least restrictive environment?"

A pall fell over the room. Because of the test results, the team felt caught in a bureaucratic Catch-22. John's IQ scores were too low to categorize him as learning disabled and too high to categorize him as educable mentally retarded. As a result, he didn't qualify for resource room services in this system where such help was traditionally reserved for those with learning disabilities.

Mark, the resource room teacher, was stunned by the irony of the situation. "How do you give extra help to the boy who is doing better and not help the child who needs it even more—just because the numbers don't fit the formula? How can I say to the parents that I'm going to help one son and not the other, especially when they're twins?"

He raised a variety of issues for the team to consider:

1. What might be the effects of moving John to the special education class now that he had already begun school?
2. The speech-language pathologist said that John needed more modeling. Perhaps children with normal language development right here could best provide this.
3. John hadn't yet received services in the least restrictive environment. It seemed like skipping a step to place him in the self-contained special education classroom without first trying to help him with resource room services from Mark in his present setting. Couldn't this be done as an academic component to his speech and language program?
4. In reviewing John's record, Mark discovered that he had been tested as a preschooler in the early intervention program. At that time, he had received a higher IQ score (107) than in the most recent test (82). Perhaps a score of 82 was a low estimate of his ability. If so, could he be considered learning disabled?
5. Were there any other services, besides resource room, available right here at Little Creek School that could give John more small group or individualized instruction?

This was a lot for the group to digest. Loretta Serkin was feeling frustrated. She wasn't sure that her class—the least restrictive environment—could meet John's needs. She wasn't concerned about having to spend extra time with John; she was more than willing to do that. She just wasn't convinced that that would do the trick. "I can provide activities for him that are at his level, but I'm afraid the other kids will see him as babyish and might begin to make fun of him. I'm not sure how that will affect his self-esteem." And she was concerned that his academic progress would be hampered as well.

Mr. D'Amico stated that they wanted John to stay at Little Creek. They understood that the school might not be able to meet all his needs academically, but they didn't want him bused to another school, The parents were aware that by third grade all programs were housed in one school which was right next door to Little Creek School. Mark thought they might be hoping to stall the need for a special placement for another year. Then, at least, the twins would be together in the same school.

"I'll work more with John at home. We can put in the extra time," Mr. D'Amico vigorously declared. Mark knew this would be an enormous effort. It was impossible to work on homework with both boys together, because David gave John the answers. They had to be helped separately.

Mrs. D'Amico's position seemed less clear-cut. She listened quietly and finally commented, "If you really feel the special class would be best for John, maybe he should go there."

The principal suggested that the team had a great deal to consider and that it would be best for everyone to have more time. He suggested that they reconvene in a week to make a decision about John's placement.

WHAT'S BEST FOR JOHN?

It was a rough week for Mark. He couldn't believe that he was hamstrung by technicalities. It seemed if a child didn't fit into a neat category, he couldn't get the services he needed. "For a specialist, it's tough. You know the child is struggling but he doesn't meet the formula, so you have to try to figure out another way to meet his needs," he told a friend. Would John's self-esteem be damaged if they removed him and put him in the self-contained classroom? Would his education be compromised if they didn't? Which was the lesser of the two evils—or was there another way out of the dilemma?

Discussion Questions

1. How do you think this problem is viewed by Mr. D'Amico? Mrs. D'Amico? Mark Reynolds? Loretta Serkin? the speech-language pathologist? John? David?
2. What are some of the underlying issues in this situation?
   • What are the ethical issues?
   • What are the practical issues?
3. Was the decision to retain the boys in first grade for a second year a good idea for John? For David? Please explain.
4. Should standardized achievement tests and intelligence tests be the primary tools used to determine a learning disability? Please explain.
5. Should schools reserve resource room help for children with learning disabilities? Why or why not? Consider the issues of demand and limited resources.

6. Consider the possible benefits of inclusion in this case. Would a collaborative model, with the various professionals working together and with John in the regular classroom, be effective?

7. John's regular education teacher points out that his lack of confidence affects both his oral and written language. Is this primarily a social-emotional problem, an academic problem, or both? Which needs to be addressed first?

8. If you were Mark, what recommendation would you make at the next PPT and why?
   - If you were Loretta Serkin, what would you suggest and why?
   - If you were Mr. or Mrs. D'Amico, what services would you want for your child?

9. In each instance in question 8, would you make the same recommendations if John were not a twin?
   - What might be the effect on David if John is transferred to another school? Has this been adequately considered?
   - What might be the effect on John if he is transferred to another school and this year is not successful for him? If he stays in the same school and if he is not successful?

10. Consider how your approach to the problems in this case would be affected if you were dealing with the same issues in a set of siblings who were not twins but whose ages were a year apart.
    - What problems might arise if one sibling is retained and ends up in the same grade as the other sibling?
    - What might be the effect on each of the siblings if one is sent to a special program in another school?

Suggested Activities

1. Role-play the final PPT meeting involving Mr. and Mrs. D'Amico, Mark, Loretta Serkin, the principal, the speech-language pathologist, and the school psychologist. Discuss and come to a decision about services for John during your role-play.

2. Interview a special education teacher. Has that teacher ever had a situation where determining a child's exceptionality in order to provide services has been difficult? How was that "case" similar to or different from this one?

3. Interview the parents of twins about the special issues with which they contend.

A s Mr. Seitz lurked outside the door and peered into the classroom, Dana Freed tried to imagine having his preschool son in her special needs class. Alex Seitz was multihandicapped. He had motor problems, speech and language difficulties, and intellectual limitations. Dana had never worked with a child who was so disabled. Although Alex posed a challenge, what really worried Dana was the prospect of having to work with Mr. Seitz.

THE SCHOOL, COMMUNITY, AND TEACHER

North Woods Elementary School was located in Amesbury, a suburban town in transition. It was once a predominately working class community, but in the past 15 years, four Fortune 500 companies had relocated there. The local factories had been replaced by sprawling corporate headquaters nestled into the hillsides. Despite the mix of white-collar professionals and "townies," Amesbury was still a close-knit community where "everybody knew everybody."

North Woods Elementary School was set off the road, surrounded by towering trees. Its spacious playground had several appealing climbers for active children to enjoy. Its classrooms were airy, with large windows looking out on the natural scene. The media center was well stocked with books and materials.

Kindergarten through fourth-grade children attended North Woods. The school had four special education classes. At the elementary level, there was a resource room for children with mild learning disabilities, Dana's class for children with severe learning disabilities, and a class for children with social-emotional problems. The town's early intervention program, a language-based preschool, was also housed there.

Dana had taught for two years before her first child was born. Several years later, when the youngest of her three children entered first grade, she returned to teaching. She had been teaching now for eleven years. Vivacious and articulate, she seemed confident of her knowledge and skills.

THE CHILD AND FAMILY

Alex was born when Bob and Leslie Seitz were in their early thirties. Both parents had a high school education, and Bob worked as an office adminstrator. They lived in a modest ranch house on the northern side of town.

Alex was born with multiple disabilities. (The Seitzes had never informed the school of the etiology, or causes, of these disabilities.) Then, a year and a half after her son was born, Leslie was diagnosed as having multiple sclerosis. Weakened by her condition, Leslie did not have the energy to devote to mothering that she would have liked. When Bob returned home from work at the end of the day, he tried to give his wife a rest, spending his time playing with the baby and attending to his needs. In time, he became Alex's primary caregiver and advocate.

At age three, Alex started the town's half-day preschool program. He received two hours a week of speech and language services in that class. He also saw the occupational therapist and the physical therapist each for one hour a week.

Alex's movements were awkward and shaky. He was unable to walk alone up the ramp to the school and had to be bolstered by two people. He needed to be belted into a special chair to sit. He spoke little, offering one word responses, if any. He had poor recall of people's faces and didn't really seem to want to interact with the other children. He had no eye contact. One of his teachers described him as "uncooperative." "He looked like he was in the group, but he was never really a part of it. He wanted to do his own thing."

THE QUESTION OF KINDERGARTEN

After spending two years in the preschool program, Alex was considered ready for kindergarten at the age of five. The planning and placement team met in the late spring to decide the best program for him. Because she wasn't Alex's teacher, Dana did not attend the meeting. However, she was very aware of the implications of the meeting for her. If Alex stayed at North Woods, he would attend Dana's special needs classroom full-time.

Dana had never worked with a child who was so disabled. "Are we equipped to help him? How can we program for him?" she wondered. Of almost greater concern was Alex's father. By now, the staff at the school was referring to him as "the stalker" because he always seemed to be hanging around, peeping into the classrooms.

The Planning and Placement Team (PPT) decided that Alex's needs would be best served at the regional educational service center about twenty miles away. The center provided programs for children with severe disabilities—primarily communication disorders—from a variety of neighboring districts.

Mr. Seitz wasn't pleased with the decision; it implied that Alex was more handicapped than he felt Alex was. However, he agreed because he needed a full-day program for his son to accommodate his work schedule. Although the North Woods kindergarten was only a half-day program, the regional center had a full-day program and transportation was provided. One day a week, the regional center was closed. On that day, Mr. Seitz arranged for Alex to attend the special needs classroom in the town next to Amesbury.

THE NEXT DECISION

For a couple of years, Dana didn't see the family. Then, one day in early January, Mr. Seitz dropped in to visit. His son was now seven years old, and he was very unhappy with the program at the regional center. He felt that Alex was not being challenged and wanted to see what the public school had to offer.

Mr. Seitz met with the principal at North Woods. He also talked with Dana and observed her classroom. It was agreed that members of the school staff should go to observe Alex at the regional center to get a clearer sense of his needs, and an appointment was quickly scheduled.

The speech-language pathologist, Dana, and Joan Edmonds, a regular education teacher, went to visit Alex the following week. Alex was now quite tall. Dana was pleased to see that Alex recognized her, even though she hadn't been his teacher at North Woods and they hadn't seen each other in a few years. In the past, Alex had had difficulty recognizing faces.

Dana saw other signs of Alex's development. For example, if the teacher asked him to point to a particular object on a page, he could do it. Mr. Seitz thought Alex was reading. Dana recognized this as   picture identification rather than real reading but, still, there was progress.

Moreover, Alex was talking a lot, although his language wasn't always appropriate. When asked a question, he often gave an unrelated answer just to respond. But it was encouraging that he was speaking, especially since the class itself didn't offer much motivation to do so. The group consisted of just five older, much bigger children who did not talk at all. Although some of their skills were more advanced than Alex's, they were using sign language. The teachers had taught Alex sign language and expected him to use it to communicate with them. At first he balked but eventually he complied.

It was obvious to Dana and the other professionals that this program clearly was not appropriate for Alex. Dana commented, "Now we weren't asking *if* we had a place. We were thinking we'll have to *make* a place. He was ready to make friends and to be part of his hometown community again."

The PPT met again and agreed to begin the transition. Alex would spend the one day a week that the regional program was closed in a first-grade classroom in North Woods School. He would continue at the regional center for the other four days.

The North Woods staff carefully considered who should be Alex's teacher. They decided upon Joan, who was welcoming, flexible, and interested in working with children with special needs. An aide was also hired to work full-time with Alex during that one day, because his safety was a concern. He was still wobbly and could easily be knocked over by other children. When he became excited, he would try to run, and then trip. The team arranged for him to arrive early and leave late to avoid the crowds of children at arrival and departure times.

GIVE HIM AN INCH, HE TAKES A MILE

The school had acted very quickly to accommodate Alex. Only a week after Mr. Seitz's visit, Alex started first grade one day a week at North Woods School. Dana, as the case manager in charge of Alex's program, was pleased with the team's efforts.

"Then, on Alex's first day here, I got a call from Mr. Seitz," Dana recalled. "He wanted Alex's regular kindergarten teacher, her aide, the resource teacher, and me to meet with him at 8:00 in the evening to fill us in about Alex's needs! Apparently, an earlier meeting wasn't convenient because of his work schedule. Joan, the regular teacher, who had only been teaching for two years, was all ready to meet at that time. But I wasn't sure this was a smart thing to do. I thought it might set a bad precedent, and I wasn't sure what he'd ask for next. It seemed like if you gave him an inch, he asked for a mile."

Despite these concerns, the teachers scheduled a special evening meeting "just this once." Luckily, according to Dana, Mr. Seitz didn't request one again. However, in April, about two months after Alex had started at North Woods, he called the school and asked to increase Alex's days at North Woods from one day to two or three. The PPT met to discuss this and decided to allow Alex to come one additional day a week.

By early June, Alex was attending North Woods three days a week. He spent all of his time in the regular first-grade class and had adapted well with the help of a full-time aide. Although Dana didn't teach Alex directly, she consulted with Joan and the aide. She provided them with all kinds of appealing materials to help Alex learn to identify colors and letters and to develop an understanding of number concepts such as one-to-one correspondence. Dana labeled all of the materials carefully and showed Joan and the aide how to use them with Alex.

The district also purchased for Alex a computer with an adaptive keyboard having larger, clearly separated letters. The special program on the computer delayed the key repeat function, so that even if Alex didn't get off a key quickly, a letter was not repeated. Alex was beginning to write his name and simple words on the computer. He was still receiving physical therapy, occupational therapy, and speech-language therapy.

Joan had done a good job of preparing the children in the class to welcome Alex, and they included him in their play. Although his language was not always appropriate, he was eager to communicate and very friendly. By June, Alex was even beginning to get invited to some birthday parties. The social benefits of inclusion for him were apparent.

The academic benefits weren't as clear initially. As Dana said, Alex was focusing on "how to do school." He was, for example, now managing in a group, walking down the hall with others, and generally complying with the rules. He was fitting in.

WHAT ABOUT NEXT YEAR?

At the June meeting of the planning and placement team, Mr. Seitz made a new demand. He was delighted and grateful that Alex was doing so well at North Woods and had decided that Alex should be there full-time in the fall. He didn't think his son needed special services at the regional center anymore.

The team was torn. They felt that Mr. Seitz's expectations of Alex were unrealistic. For example, he was convinced that Alex had actually been reading at the regional program when, in fact, he was just picture reading. In just a few months, he wanted Alex switched from an entirely self-contained program to one of full inclusion. He did still want his son to have physical therapy, occupational therapy, and speech therapy.

Moreover, he insisted that his son be placed with the same teacher, Joan, because Alex had become quite attached to her. Since Joan was "moving up" to work in a mixed age classroom, this might be feasible. The team members decided they needed some time to weigh the pros and cons of Mr. Seitz's request.

Dana felt pressured, knowing that they would be relying on her judgment. She had two children with disabilities (Alex and John), and two classrooms at that level in which to place them. Each of them had an aide. It looked like Alex could be in Joan's class, but then another complication arose.

GOING TO THE TOP

Dana received notice that another student, Julia, who was also severely disabled, was going to be coming to North Woods in the fall. Julia needed an aide, too. Unfortunately, the district did not have the money to hire three aides.

The placement process began to seem like a confusing puzzle to Dana. She tried mixing and matching the two teachers, two aides, and three children in various combinations. She had to be careful not to overload either teacher. She finally determined that it would be in the best interests of all three children with disabilities, as well as the other children in the classes, to place Julia and John with one aide in Joan's class. Alex and his aide would be in the other class. Then the phone rang.

The director of pupil personnel, her boss, was on the line. The director had just received a call from the superintendent of schools. Apparently, Mr. Seitz had called the superintendent to insist that Alex be permitted to come to North Woods full-time and be placed with Joan in the fall. The superintendent had said to the director, "Why don't you make him happy? Let's not make waves."

Dana's blood began to boil. She couldn't believe that this parent had gone all the way to the top! Then again, why should she be surprised—he'd been pushing every step of the way. Now, what should she do?

Discussion Questions

1. What is Dana's immediate dilemma at the end of the case?
2. What are the underlying issues in this situation?
3. How might the situation look from the points of view of Dana? Joan? Mr. Seitz? Alex? The school superintendent?
4. Why does Dana feel that Mr. Seitz has been "pushing every step of the way?" Give some specific examples.
   - Do you feel that his requests are appropriate or inappropriate? Consider Alex's abilities and needs and the resources and limitations at North Woods.
   - Would Alex have progressed as well if Mr. Seitz had not advocated so strongly for him?
5. Should Dana have set clearer limits for Mr. Seitz? If so, at what point and how?
6. What are the potential advantages of full inclusion? What are the potential disadvantages?
7. Chart the changes in Dana's outlook on having Alex in her class and in her school.
8. If you were Dana, what would you do at the end of the case and why?

Suggested Activities

1. Role-play the telephone conversation between Dana and the director of pupil personnel. Role-play the conversation a second time and reverse roles, so that you and your partner can represent both perspectives.
2. Identify a school that has implemented full inclusion for some of its students. Interview a regular teacher and a special education teacher in that

school. Based upon their experiences, what do they see as the advantages of full inclusion? What do they see as the disadvantages? How have they worked together? Report your findings to the class.

3. Identify advocacy groups for parents of children with disabilities in your community. Interview representatives from the groups. What services do they provide? From their perspective, how is the group most needed? Write a pamphlet describing these services in the community, which a teacher could share with parents.

High Hopes

CHARACTERS

Special education teacher:	Janice Davis
Classroom aide and	
first-grade teacher:	Marsha Mann
Second-grade teacher:	Elaine Jordan
Student:	Ronald Stallings
Parents:	Jerome and Ruth Stallings

Janice Davis, a special educator, had been teaching Ronald Stallings, a second grader with hydrocephalus, since he started kindergarten at Pine Woods Elementary School.

Ronald had visual-perceptual difficulties and motor problems that made it hard for him to learn to write. His letters were large and sprawled across the page, and it took him forever to finish an assignment. Luckily, the school provided a computer keyboard adapted to his needs, with very large, clearly separated letters. He managed it well. But his mother still hoped that he would be able to write like the other children. And this was representative of the problem, as Janice related it to her husband one Sunday evening.

"A few days ago, Mrs. Stallings begged me again to require Ronald to handwrite each of his spelling words. I hate to ask Ronald to do it. It's frustrating for him and not even necessary since he has the computer. I don't think he'll ever be able to handwrite to meet his daily needs like the other children, but I can't seem to get his parents to see that."

THE SCHOOL, COMMUNITY, AND TEACHER

Pine Woods Elementary School was located in the town of Hightstown, a community of about 50,000 residents of varied ethnic and racial backgrounds. Pine Woods was the school with the wealthiest population and the highest standardized test scores in the town. Many fathers were lawyers, doctors, businessmen, and consultants. Mothers often stayed home with their children; those who worked outside of the home tended to be very busy with prestigious jobs.

Although the school was 25 years old, its sprawling modern structure looked brand new compared to many of the schools in the town. It had about 300 children in its kindergarten through second grades. Its special services included a resource room teacher who worked primarily with children having learning disabilities, a full-time reading specialist, a school psychologist (two days a week), a social worker (one day a week), a speech-language pathologist (two and a half days a week), an occupational therapist and physical therapist as needed for individual children, and Janice.

Janice Davis had been teaching for four years, all at Pine Woods. Ronald's kindergarten year had been her second year of teaching. Janice majored in special education as an undergraduate, and she specialized in learning disabilities at the master's level. Now she primarily worked with children with more severe disabilities. She and the reading specialist shared a room where children came for individual and small group instruction a few hours a day. She also worked with children in their regular classrooms.

A tall woman with long dark hair, Janice saw working with parents as crucial to her role as a teacher. Her eyes twinkled when she talked about her work. She wanted parents as partners, making joint decisions with her about their children. She didn't want to impose her ideas; in fact, she felt a teacher-directed approach was likely to backfire.

She taught eight to 12 children a year. Each month, she made it a point to call every parent. During this personal contact, she gave parents a progress report on their children and asked if they had any questions. Although she occasionally would write "good news" notes, she didn't want to express concerns about a child in writing since these might be misunderstood. In such cases, she liked to speak with the parents directly. As a result of her policy of frequent communication, parents rarely came to her to complain. "I've gone to them before they come to me," she commented. These calls were so important that she always made them, even during the year her father was very ill and she was driving an hour each day to visit him in the hospital.

THE CHILD AND FAMILY

Ronald was an African-American child of average height and weight. At age seven, the only sign of his disability was his slightly larger head. At birth, however, it was obvious that he had hydrocephalus, a condition in which cerebrospinal fluid accumulates in the brain. He had needed several operations, first to implant a shunt and then to drain the fluid and to ensure that it was working properly.

The Stallings family had lived in Hightstown for several years. Both parents were accountants, and Ronald was their only child. Before his birth,

Mrs. Stallings had worked full-time in an accounting firm, and she returned to work part-time when Ronald entered kindergarten.

Always impeccably dressed, Mrs. Stallings had a real knack for business. To Janice, she seemed confident and efficient, and she was certainly used to making her own decisions. Although she had returned to work, she remained very involved in her son's education. She picked Ronald up from school every day and often touched base with his teachers to see how Ronald was doing.

When Ronald was born, Mrs. Stallings was 30 years old and Mr. Stallings was 32. They had been married for seven years. Although both parents were obviously distressed by Ronald's hydrocephalus, Mr. Stallings seemed to take it much harder. Unlike most parents, he didn't proudly announce the birth of his son. Mrs. Stallings was left with the responsibility for scheduling all of Ronald's medical appointments and getting him to them. However, by the end of the first year, she felt that her husband had grown more accepting of his son's condition.

When Ronald was two and a half, he started to attend the town's early intervention preschool program. There he received physical and occupational therapy to strengthen his body, improve his balance, and help him walk more steadily. The Stallings paid for extra OT and PT services at home during the year and throughout the summer.

In the spring before Ronald entered kindergarten, Mr. and Mrs. Stallings came to visit the school and to discuss services that would be available for their son. Janice noted to herself that these were conscientious parents. They insisted on being well informed and involved.

KINDERGARTEN

Ronald was identified as multihandicapped. He received special services for his physical disability, visual-perceptual problems, motor problems, and language problems. Although he was talking, he had difficulty with the subtleties of language, such as verb tenses. Moreover, he tended to give one-word responses, speaking in full sentences only when prompted. He saw an occupational therapist for three half-hour individual sessions a week and a physical therapist for two half-hour individual sessions a week.

Ronald was placed in a regular half-day kindergarten, and Janice worked primarily in the regular class with Ronald. Ronald was often alone, and Janice's goal was to help him to interact comfortably with others. He played near other children, but not with them. He was so used to individual attention that he often wasn't aware of the group. When he failed to follow the teacher's directions and join the group at meeting time, Janice helped him. Moreover, his body wasn't strong, so sometimes he just couldn't keep up with the other children. On the playground, he was often left behind as the other children raced around.

In addition to working with Janice in the kindergarten, Ronald went to Janice's room to focus on motor and beginning readiness skills for about 30 minutes each day. They worked on letter and number formation through a multisensory approach, for example by painting the letters and numbers. Ronald knew the letter names but not their sounds, so Janice helped him with that through many rhyming activities. They read preprimers and told stories.

Initially, Ronald was not assigned an aide. Although his head was slightly larger than usual, he looked normal. However, Ronald was wobbly. He couldn't step up a stair or maintain his balance on the playground's sand or when turning around in the bathroom. If someone bumped him, he might topple over. He couldn't carry a tray at lunchtime. Ronald was at risk of hurting himself—and if he hit his head, he might disturb the shunt. Janice quickly saw these problems and sent her own aide to work with Ronald.

By late October, Ronald was assigned his own full-time aide, Marsha Mann, for safety reasons. Marsha was a certified teacher and also helped Ronald academically. Since Ronald wasn't used to being part of a large group he often tuned out, engaging instead in self-stimulating activities such as head rocking. Marsha helped him to focus.

Mrs. Stallings managed to visit every day, volunteering to help the teacher prepare art materials or plan field trips. At some point during the day, she'd stop Janice to talk about Ronald. "Do you have a minute. . . .?" she'd preface her comment or question. Janice would respond, "Yes, I do, but can you call me or make an appointment?" While she wanted to be available to parents, she felt they needed to learn that she couldn't talk with them during instructional time.

Mrs. Stallings also wanted Janice to keep a daily notebook on Ronald's progress, as teachers had done in the preschool. The teachers wrote daily notes to parents, and parents could respond. The child carried the notebook to and from school. Again, Janice needed to set a limit. "I wish I could do that, Mrs. Stallings, but I'm responsible for more children than the preschool teachers were. If I spend time every day writing about your child, I'll have less time to actually work with him," she explained. Mrs. Stallings nodded and never raised the issue again.

TRANSITION PROGRAM

After kindergarten, Ronald was placed in the transition program to give him extra time to develop in all ways. He also spent three hours a day in Janice's room working on reading, written expression, and mathematics. He was mainstreamed into the regular classroom for instruction in science, social studies, art, music, and gym, as well as play time. The physical therapist and occupational therapist continued to work with him.

Ronald had a good visual memory and appeared to be learning to read. He knew the alphabet in kindergarten and could even spell some words in preschool and kindergarten. Mrs. Stallings would proudly tell Ronald to "read" a word for Janice, and Ronald would name the letters.

However, Ronald had difficulty writing and his letters were very large. He practiced his printing intently during one-to-one and small group situations with Janice, using a slant board to assist him with the angle. The slant board also helped him visually by bringing the print closer to his eyes. Nevertheless, he couldn't handwrite in a way that was functional. Janice was delighted when the school purchased a computer keyboard adapted to suit Ronald's needs, but Mrs. Stallings still pleaded, "Can't you teach him to write like the other children?"

Since the school was about half a mile from the center of town, the children often walked there on field trips. During his preschool years, Ronald had been pulled in a wagon. By the middle of kindergarten, however, Janice felt that this was inappropriate. Wagons were typically used by much younger children.

In April, the children in the transition class were taking a walking trip to the grocery store. The transition teacher didn't think Ronald would have the stamina to make this trek, so she asked Mrs. Stallings to give Ronald a ride. Mrs. Stallings reacted strongly. She wanted Ronald to be with the rest of the children, and she suggested that he be pulled by the aide in the wagon.

The transition teacher consulted with Janice, and Janice called Mrs. Stallings. She explained that the wagon wasn't feasible or safe. Ronald was too heavy for the aide to pull him, and he might topple over in the wagon. Moreover, the other children would consider it "babyish." Either Mrs. Stallings could drive Ronald or Ronald would be pushed by the aide in a wheelchair. Mrs. Stallings balked at the suggestion of the wheelchair.

"It's up to you," Janice gently explained. "But if he were my child, I'd want him to be pushed in a wheelchair with the group. Once he gets downtown, he can walk. Think it over and call me back." Two days later, Mrs. Stallings called Janice and agreed to the wheelchair, but Janice could tell she wasn't happy.

FIRST GRADE

Janice saw less of Mrs. Stallings when Ronald was in first grade. Marsha Mann, the certified teacher who had been Ronald's aide since kindergarten, was hired as a first-grade teacher and Ronald was placed in her class. Since Marsha knew Ronald so well, Mrs. Stallings seemed relaxed and confident about Ronald's education.

At the end of first grade, it was time for Ronald's triennial evaluation, and Janice decided to request an IQ test for Ronald. By this time, Ronald's reading was problematic. "If you hear him read, you think he's a good little reader, but he's a 'word caller.' He's not really reading," Janice told the school psychologist. Ronald had difficulty with tracking and comprehension. He could tell you the name of a character, but he couldn't predict what would happen next in a story. Similarly, he knew number facts but had trouble with problem solving in math. And his response time was very slow. Sometimes Janice had to wait as long as five minutes for even a one word answer from Ronald.

Mrs. Stallings had always said how smart Ronald was, and the other teachers were impressed by him. He was verbal and when he spoke to teachers in the hall, he'd say something cute or catchy. However, Janice realized that he often repeated these expressions over and over.

At each of the report card conferences, Janice had been trying to lay the groundwork to help the Stallingss develop more realistic expectations. When she described Ronald's reading, Mr. Stallings responded, "Ronald's smart. He can learn anything. You just have to be patient and teach him. Please don't give up on him." He often worked with Ronald at home, and Janice wondered whether he ever became impatient with his son. Janice had no intention of giving up, but she wanted to be realistic.

Mrs. Stallings asked, "But he's made progress, hasn't he?" Although Ronald had made progress, Janice tried to help them to see that his level of reading wasn't typical for his age. Both parents wanted suggestions as to how they could help Ronald more at home. Sometimes Janice wondered what the pediatrician had said to them at Ronald's birth about his potential. Had he led them to expect too little or too much?

In May, before Ronald's regularly scheduled planning and placement team meeting to plan for the next year, a conference was held to discuss the IQ test results. The school psychologist, Janice, Marsha, and Mr. and Mrs. Stallings were present. When the psychologist explained that Ronald's IQ was in the low to average range (84), Mrs. Stallings' eyes welled with tears and she said, "But he's doing so much better than I ever thought he would. I'm just happy if he makes progress every year." Mr. Stallings listened, but Janice wasn't sure that he really understood.

SECOND GRADE

In first grade, Ronald had developed a friendship with another little boy. At Mrs. Stallings' request, Janice arranged for the boys to be placed in the same second grade. Ronald was also beginning to form other relationships and, to help her son socialize more, Mrs. Stallings became a group leader for the Cub Scouts.

Janice felt that second grade was Ronald's best year yet. As a team, Janice, the aide, and Ronald's regular teacher, Elaine Jordan, worked to involve Ronald more and more as a member of the group. They didn't want Ronald to be "out of it," waiting for individual help all of the time. When Elaine asked the children to put on their coats and line up, Ronald needed to keep pace and not wait for an individual cue. Now he had the physical strength to keep up, but he still liked to be babied. "You can do it. Go along," everyone encouraged him. The aide began to spend more time with the other children so that Ronald would develop independence.

In addition to helping Ronald in the regular classroom, Janice taught Ronald two hours each day in the special education room. They worked on reading, writing on the computer, and math. The computer keyboard traveled back and forth with Ronald between the regular classroom and Janice's room. Mrs. Stallings still occasionally asked Janice to help Ronald practice his handwriting.

Outdoors, Ronald couldn't keep up with the children's running, but now some kids joined him in the sandbox. He even began to pull himself onto the climber when it wasn't too crowded.

The physical therapist and occupational therapist worked with Ronald, as always. The physical therapist was helping him learn to climb a small set of three to four stairs. He could now climb up but not down.

CHOOSING THE NEXT SCHOOL

There were four schools, at opposite ends of town, for grades three to five in Hightstown. The children from Pine Woods typically went to the one nearby, a two-story brick building that was the oldest school in the district. One of the schools at the other end of town was a modern one-story structure. By law, the town was required to make only one of the schools accessible to children with disabilities.

Mrs. Stallings had been talking about placing Ronald in the two-story school, but Janice couldn't imagine Ronald managing those flights of stairs and there was no elevator. However, at the one-story school, Ronald, who was just beginning to make friends, wouldn't know any children. And his mother, who was very active in the PTA, wouldn't know any parents. There were clear disadvantages to both schools for Ronald and his family.

Janice knew that Mrs. Stallings wanted her child to be like everyone else. And, goodness knows, she had been very attentive in trying to help her son. But it just wasn't going to happen. Could Janice help Mrs. Stallings to adjust her expectations again?

Discussion Questions

1. What is Janice's dilemma?
2. Evaluate Janice's strategies for communicating with parents. How effective were these?
   - Do you agree with Janice that a teacher-directed approach to working with parents is likely to backfire? Please explain.
   - Did Janice leave too much of the decision making up to the Stallings? Please explain.

3. What requests did Mr. and Mrs. Stallings make of the school? Were these appropriate, inadequate, or excessive? Support your response.
4. As a teacher, how does one determine realistic expectations for a child?
   • What are the risks of setting one's sights too low?
   • What are the risks of setting one's sights too high?
5. What were Mr. and Mrs. Stallings expectations for Ronald? Were these realistic or not? What factors might be influencing these? Please explain your response.
6. What kinds of expectations are typical for a parent to have of a child with disabilities?
   • Can you generalize about this?
   • How can you help parents to develop appropriate expectations?
7. The Stallings would like Ronald to "fit in." Do schools sometimes comply with this desire that parents of children with special needs may have? If so, in what ways do schools attempt to minimize differences among children?
8. If you were Janice, what would you do at the end of the case?
9. The Stallings live in a moderately wealthy school district. If this were a poorer school district, would your recommendations be different? Please explain.

Suggested Activities

1. Role-play a conference to discuss which school Ronald should go to next year. Determine who the participants should be and role-play their varying perspectives.
2. Review the research and write a paper on stages of parental reaction to a child's disability.
3. Read three to four books written by or for parents of children with physical disabilities. Develop an annotated bibliography you could share with parents.

The Case of Neglect

CHARACTERS

Special education teacher:	Tyrone Forbes
Second- and third-grade teacher:	Evelyn Simpson
Social worker:	Jane Freeman
Student's mentor:	Hilda Forman
Student:	Anita Suggs
Parents:	Emma Suggs and James Campbell

Tyrone Forbes, the special education teacher, and Jane Freeman, the school social worker, pulled up in front of the two-story townhouse where Anita Suggs and her family lived. They were making a home visit to try to establish contact with Anita's mother and to encourage her to send her daughter to school on a regular basis. It was early December, and Anita, who had transferred to Lincoln School in late October, was repeating first grade. At her previous school, she had a record of very poor attendance, which may have been the cause of her academic difficulties.

They rang the doorbell several times, wondering whether it worked. Since it was late morning, the family should have been up. The house's peeling paint gave it a careworn appearance. Finally, the door was cracked open a few inches. A tall woman, looking like she had just awakened, peered through the chained space. "Who is it?" she asked gruffly. Tyrone and Jane quickly identified themselves, hoping to be let in so they could talk to Anita's mother face to face. Ms. Suggs opened the door wide but stood at the threshold, waiting impatiently for them to continue. Casting their eyes around the room, Tyrone and Jane noted that it was sparsely furnished.

Trying to be friendly and nonthreatening, Tyrone and Jane explained how important it was for Anita to attend school regularly in order for her to advance. There was standardized testing being conducted now, and she needed to take the tests, as well as participate in the other school experiences.

Ms. Suggs responded angrily. "You school people. You're always looking for problems. We haven't done anything; you have no right to bother me!" she shouted and closed the door.

THE SCHOOL, COMMUNITY, AND TEACHER

Lincoln Elementary School was one of twenty-five elementary schools in the city of Eastport, which had about 130,000 residents. Although located in one of the country's wealthiest states, it was ranked as the nation's seventh-poorest city. It once had thriving industries, particularly in the tool and die trade, but there was now a high rate of unemployment. Several colleges and universities, two hospitals, and some insurance companies were the city's major employers. In per-pupil spending for education, Eastport ranked last in the state.

The city had social problems typical of many urban areas. A recent survey had rated it as one of the more dangerous places to live in the United States. In some neighborhoods there was rampant drug trafficking and gang warfare; many parents would not let their children play outdoors, fearing they would be caught in street violence. Children as young as ten were being recruited by gangs with the lure of easy money. With its high rate of IV drug use, Eastport also had a high rate of AIDS infection.

Lincoln School had about 500 children in its kindergarten through sixth grades. Eighty percent of the children were African-American and 20 percent were Hispanic. About half of the teachers were African-American and half were white. It was located in an area of the city that was poor but relatively safe.

Because of its excellent reputation, many parents, particularly professionals, chose Lincoln for their children. The students were expected to wear uniforms and to be well disciplined. The school community was proud of its excellent music program. The principal was admired by parents, children, and the teaching staff. An energetic, endlessly positive woman, she had personal connections throughout the community, which she frequently drew on to help students.

As Tyrone pointed out, "She'll go to the nth degree for the children. Whenever we think we're stuck in terms of helping a child, she'll start calling around. She'll call anyone—the Department of Children and Families, the local alderman, the child's pediatrician. She never gives up and she's more than willing to stick her neck out. The teachers know she's behind the kids 100 percent."

Tyrone Forbes was another person who was willing to stick his neck out for kids. As the resource room teacher, he worked primarily with children with learning disabilities. He taught at Lincoln School each week for three days and at another elementary school for two days. Children generally came to him for individualized instruction in academics. He often consulted with the regular education teachers and suggested strategies to them as well. In addition to

Tyrone, other special services included a school social worker and school psychologist each for two days a week, a speech-language pathologist for one and a half days a week, and a school nurse for one day a week.

Tyrone had been teaching for eight years. Originally trained as a regular education teacher, he had taught for a year in an elementary school. During that first year, he had a student who received help from the resource room teacher. "I was at a loss as to how to help her myself," he commented, "and I wanted to be able to." When he needed to get his master's degree to retain his certification, he enrolled in a special education program. Most of his career had been spent as a special educator.

THE CHILD AND FAMILY

Anita Suggs was petite for her seven years. She had been born prematurely, only 16 months after her older brother, Charles. Her mother and father had never married, and the children lived with their mother. Emma Suggs was on public assistance.

Tyrone had the feeling that Ms. Suggs favored Anita's brother. Although Tyrone described Anita as "pretty and just the sweetest child," Ms. Suggs had said she "looked just like her father and wasn't much smarter." Both children had had poor attendance records and academic problems, but Charles seemed to find school somewhat easier.

FIRST GRADE

After transferring to Lincoln, Anita repeated first grade. She was not reading at all, and her overall academic skills were poor. She was often truant at her previous school, and her teacher at Lincoln wasn't sure if her poor performance was caused by low ability or simply by lack of exposure to the skills and concepts.

The staff at Lincoln worked to get Anita to come to school on a regular basis. Usually parents purchased the school uniform, but the principal provided one for Anita. Both the principal and Anita's teacher called and wrote to Ms. Suggs several times to remind her to send her child to school. Sometimes no one answered the phone. A few of the letters got returned—the Suggs family moved frequently from one housing situation to another and would forget to notify the school. Despite the school's efforts, Anita was still often absent. When she *was* at school, she was well behaved and got along with the other students, but she rarely spoke in class.

By mid-February, Anita had missed 20 days of school. Her academic performance was below grade level in all areas. Because of the number of days absent, the school was legally required to identify Anita's family as "a family with service needs" to the juvenile court system. The Planning and Placement

Team had to complete the required forms. Ms. Suggs was invited to the team's meeting, but she did not attend. By the terms of the state truancy policy, the team was required to hold the meeting without her.

The team didn't like to take legal action—it was usually the course of last resort—but they did. When Tyrone reflected on the situation later, he noted ironically that it was a useless move. The court took no noticeable action at all. Maybe the papers were lost in the shuffle.

SECOND GRADE

The school staff resolved to keep a close eye on Anita. Although her second-grade teacher, Evelyn Simpson, was well-meaning and kept talking about referring Anita for an evaluation, she never did.

In the middle of second grade, something good happened to Anita. The school had a mentor program that paired students with adults for attention, encouragement, and occasionally academic help. The mentor might be an adult from the community or a nearby business, or a teacher in the school.

In Anita's case, one of the parents, Hilda Forman, who volunteered at Lincoln, noticed that the young girl needed help and asked to be her mentor. An officer in the Parent-Teacher Organization, Hilda believed that her own child would do better academically if she were a strong presence in the school. Her part-time work schedule gave her the time to volunteer frequently.

Hilda was outraged that this shy, quiet child, who seemed so lost, was not getting extra assistance. Anita's attendance had improved, but she was still far behind the other children academically. "This is a crime," Hilda commented to Tyrone. "Let's get moving." Together, they asked the second-grade teacher to submit the necessary papers for a referral. Evelyn Simpson responded defensively to Tyrone, "I thought I gave them to you weeks ago. You must have lost them."

Finally, by the end of second grade, Evelyn completed the necessary forms, and Tyrone sent an invitation to Ms. Suggs to attend a planning and placement team meeting to discuss her daughter's needs.

Once again, Ms. Suggs failed to attend. Although the team members were required by their supervisors to hold the meeting anyway, they decided to reschedule it with the hope that they could get Ms. Suggs involved. But they were not successful.

THIRD GRADE

Evelyn Simpson was given permission to "move up" with her entire second-grade class to third grade, so Anita would be in her class again. "She can't do anything," Evelyn Simpson complained about Anita. Anita still wasn't reading or writing yet. Her math skills were almost on grade level; she could add and subtract.

The staff wanted to conduct a psychoeducational and social work assessment of Anita. They scheduled a planning and placement team meeting in early November and invited Ms. Suggs, but she failed to show up. By this time, the team recognized the urgency of holding the PPT anyway to formally request an evaluation of Anita, and so they met.

Then they needed Ms. Suggs's permission to conduct the testing. At this point, Tyrone grabbed the social worker. "Let's just go to Anita's house to find Ms. Suggs and get her to sign the form," he urged. "I wish I could but I just can't take the time," responded the social worker. "I'm working in three different schools, and my case load is overwhelming."

A few days later, Ms. Suggs dropped by Evelyn Simpson's class—a rare occurrence. Taking advantage of the opportunity, Evelyn asked the mother to stop by Tyrone's room to sign the form, and she did.

Arrangements for the evaluation could now be made. The social worker would conduct the family component, which included interviews with the parent about the child's medical history, developmental milestones, and family life. She would also talk with Anita and observe her in her class. The school psychologist would conduct the psychoeducational assessment.

The speech-language pathologist was responsible for the language component. Unfortunately, she wanted to postpone it. "I'm too busy. Don't put me down for an observation yet," she entreated. Tyrone felt this was unconscionable. After all, Anita was virtually mute. But administrative regulations made it impossible for the school to engage someone else to carry out the assessment.

THE UP SIDE

In some ways, things began to turn around for Anita in third grade. Her father, James Campbell, began to take an interest in her. He came to school once a week and read a story to the children, and Anita listened proudly.

Hilda also became more involved with Anita. She stopped by Evelyn's class every day to say hi and give Anita a warm hug. Two or three times a month, she worked with Anita in the classroom, reading with her or helping her with other assignments.

Anita participated in school performances. The music teacher was a caring, enthusiastic person who promoted a sense of pride and camaraderie. With her encouragement, Anita began to open up. She was using her voice to sing and was learning new words for songs. She began to talk more now.

THE DOWN SIDE

Emma Suggs was furious that Anita's father had been coming to see her at school. "I don't want him here. I'm gonna get a court order," she threatened. She bristled even more when Anita brought home a doll that her father had bought her. But she never did get the court order; Tyrone wasn't sure whether she even had sole custody of Anita.

In December, Anita's class performed in the holiday assembly. This was a special evening event, but Ms. Suggs insisted that Anita go to a party with her instead. Anita begged her mother to take her to the performance, but her mother still said no.

In January, for the big concert to celebrate Martin Luther King, Jr. Day, Hilda bought Anita a beautiful new dress. It was an opportunity for Anita to shine, but her mother didn't come to the concert.

THE PLANNING AND PLACEMENT TEAM MEETING

In early January, the PPT met to discuss the results of Anita's psychoeducational evaluation and the social worker's report. The social worker was pleased that she had been able to arrange a meeting with Ms. Suggs and had obtained the necessary information.

The school psychologist's testing revealed that there was a significant difference between Anita's verbal and performance scores on the IQ test. Furthermore, academically, she was one to one and a half years below her grade level. As a result, she qualified for services as a student with learning disabilities. However, a speech-language evaluation was needed to determine if she might qualify for Direct Language Therapy. The speech-language pathologist still hadn't scheduled the assessment, in part because Ms. Suggs had to give permission for it to be carried out.

The team's level of frustration reached new heights. The members couldn't believe they'd come this far and couldn't yet give Anita the help she needed. During lunchtime, Tyrone was telling Hilda what had happened, and Hilda was flabbergasted. "This is ridiculous. Let's go to the house right now," she insisted. Although he had another child he was supposed to work with right then, Tyrone decided to drop everything and go.

Fortunately, Ms. Suggs was home. She claimed that she had never received any of the invitations to any of the PPTs she had missed. "You probably mailed them to the wrong address," she angrily accused Tyrone. Although she signed the necessary permission for the language evaluation, she threatened them on the way out. "Don't ever show your face at my house again or you'll be sorry!" she shouted.

THE SAGA CONTINUES

Even with the appropriate parental permission, the speech-language pathologist did not conduct the evaluation. Tyrone couldn't stand it anymore. This child had been in their school for over a year and a half, and she still wasn't getting the help she needed. "Sometimes teaching has to be a subversive activity," Tyrone told his wife.

From his professional experience, he was quite sure that Anita would ultimately be identified as learning disabled. In the past months, he had observed her informally in her classroom and occasionally sat with her to give her some help. "Your conscience tells you that you must know this child. You can't sit through a PPT and be totally unfamiliar with the child."

Now he decided to go even further. Even though Anita had not been formally identified, he invited her to come to the resource room a few times when the two other students from her class, who had been identified, came. He and Anita became friends, and Tyrone began to give her at least some of the help she needed.

Another PPT, Late February

The speech-language pathologist finally completed her evaluation of Anita, and the team was ready to hold another PPT. Emma Suggs was invited to the meeting but she did not come.

The school psychologist reviewed the results from the psychoeducational and language testing and concluded that Anita qualified for special education services as a learning disabled child. No speech-language services were warranted. The social worker's report indicated that Anita had a low self-image. Then the team developed an individualized education plan that prescribed the following services:

1. Resource room services: 6 hours per week
2. Social work services: 1/2 hour per week in school

There was just one final hurdle to be overcome. Ms. Suggs had to give permission for Anita finally to get help. "How are we going to get that?" Tyrone asked despairingly.

Discussion Questions

1. What is Tyrone's immediate problem?
2. What are the underlying issues in this situation?
3. When Anita was in second grade, should the PPT have postponed their meeting, given Ms. Suggs's history so far? Please explain your decision.
4. Were home visits an effective strategy in this case? What other approaches might have been tried?
5. In early November of Anita's third-grade year, the PPT formally requested an evaluation of her. The team did not reconvene to discuss the results of the evaluation and plan for services until early January. Why? Was this legal? Is such a lengthy delay characteristic in schools? What can be done to avoid a time lag of this sort so services are delivered in a more timely manner?
6. Was the parent volunteer, Hilda, helpful? Why or why not?

- Was she overstepping her boundaries as a volunteer? As the parent of another child?
- Should the staff have enlisted her help in other ways? If so, how?

7. Tyrone states, "Sometimes teaching has to be a subversive activity." What do you think he meant?
    - Do you agree? Please explain your thinking.
    - In what ways did Tyrone carry out this statement?
    - Was he justified in giving services to Anita before Anita was formally identified?
    - If the school had more of an inclusion model, might Tyrone have worked more informally with Anita sooner?

8. Can a school provide services to a child if the parent either actively or passively refuses them?
    - In this situation, was there any other recourse?
    - What if legal measures are not effective?

9. Who, if anyone, was neglectful in this case? Might there be systemic neglect and not just personal neglect here?

10. What should the professional staff do at the end of the case study?

Suggested Activities

1. In teams of three, role-play Tyrone and Hilda's initial home visit to Emma Suggs in early October of Anita's first-grade year. Role-play other ways in which Tyrone and Hilda might have handled the home visit.

2. Review federal and state laws that regulate special education services, including the mandated time schedules for the determination and delivery of services to a child. What legal recourse is available to schools and parents if the laws and their prescribed timetables are not followed?

3. Interview a special education teacher. Has she or he had an experience with a parent who refused to agree to an evaluation and/or services for a child? How was that situation handled?

What's Best for Jamilah?

CHARACTERS

Special education teacher:	Jenny McDowell
Student:	Jamilah Rasheed
Parents:	Jabar and Nykesha Rasheed

Jenny McDowell shook her head in amazement when the school psychologist told her about his evaluation of Jamilah Rasheed. Jamilah, a kindergartner, had a clear language disability. She spoke only two- or three-word sentences and couldn't carry on a conversation. She often echoed others' words. Yet, as the psychologist was testing her, she was fluently reading his manual upside down!

THE SCHOOL, COMMUNITY, AND TEACHER

Garland Elementary School was in Grant, a city of about 110,000 people. Having lost its original manufacturing base when the garment industry moved out, the city had been struggling with little success for several years to entice high-technology businesses to settle there. The population was increasingly poor. Because the tax base had eroded, there was intense competition among city agencies for the limited funding available.

Garland School was located in a shoreline-section of the city. Its massive two-story brick building had housed three generations of children. A neighborhood school, it drew children primarily from the surrounding working-class community. There were approximately 300 children in its kindergarten through fourth grades. The children came from diverse backgrounds; about 100 were African-American, 50 were Hispanic, and 150 were Caucasian.

Garland had extensive special education services for children. There were three self-contained special education classrooms, two of which were for children with language disabilities. These were the only classrooms in the city designed to meet the needs of children whose language disabilities were so extreme that they could not attend regular classrooms. However, because the children's IQs were high enough, with help they had the potential of moving into the mainstream. The third classroom was for children who were both language disabled and mildly mentally retarded. In addition, a resource room teacher, speech-language pathologist, occupational therapist, and physical therapist were available as needed for all the schoolchildren.

Jenny McDowell taught one of the classes for children with language disabilities. The class had 12 children from both first and second grades, as well as a part-time aide.

Jenny had been teaching for 15 years. An attractive woman in her late 30s, she exuded competence. She had a master's degree in special education and a sixth-year diploma in administration and supervision. She had taught children with special needs at both the preschool and elementary levels.

Her expertise was well respected in the community. She served on the Board of Directors for several community organizations and was sought after as a guest speaker on special needs topics. Audiences appreciated her knowledge and her lively wit.

Jenny modified the regular first- and second-grade curriculum for her students, teaching them all of the subjects. In addition to this classroom instruction, each child had one hour of speech therapy per week. The speech-language pathologist also advised Jenny on ways to focus on individual children's needs to reinforce their developing skills throughout the day. The children's language was generally delayed by two to three years.

Jenny taught language skills in a structured way. Although most children of this age were absorbing new words almost effortlessly, Jenny's kids avoided using them, so vocabulary drills were necessary. She also had to make these children conscious of rules that other children learned intuitively. When a child commented, "I got two mitten," she responded, "Oh, you have two mitten*s*," pronouncing the "s" distinctly. "'S' means you have more than one." Some of the children didn't know how to ask a question. If one said, "We will go to the gym today," with a questioning tone, Jenny would respond, "You mean, *will* we go to the gym today?" Although Jenny recognized that it was a tough call to know whether or not to interrupt a child's speech, she thought that these particular children needed to be corrected.

There were three reading groups. The children at the lower level were working on phonics lessons from the kindergarten curriculum. The middle group was working at the first-grade level, and the highest group was almost at a second-grade level.

Her classroom included learning centers, such as an art area and block corner, where children could engage in less-structured activities. This gave children an opportunity to use their new skills in informal situations. Sometimes she would pair each child with a language buddy so they could work together.

THE CHILD AND FAMILY

Jamilah had spent the first half of the kindergarten year in another school, Lincoln Elementary School. She could not be tested at the usual kindergarten screening because of her language level. During her first months in kindergarten, she was unable to learn new skills and information unless the teacher taught her individually. However, she could read. Her decoding skills were excellent, although her comprehension was not good. In addition, she was able to identify numbers through 100.

Jamilah first impressed Jenny as an appealing child who was excited about learning. She was generally sweet and cooperative, except when she was frustrated.

But she had serious language delays. She couldn't converse, couldn't answer questions, couldn't follow directions, and echoed others' words. Her attention span was short and her speech often unintelligible. Her sentences were only two or three words long. Sometimes her speech turned to gibberish when she tried to throw in extra sounds to lengthen her sentences. If Jamilah became frustrated, which was often, she would cry. Then it was even harder to understand her.

Jamilah's family lived across town. They were devout Muslims who were very concerned about their daughter's education. Jamilah had a two-year-old sister.

Mrs. Rasheed was a high school graduate and did not work outside of the home. Mr. Rasheed had graduated from the local community college and worked as a technician in a hospital. The family lived in public housing.

When Jamilah's kindergarten teacher at Lincoln School became concerned about her language, Jenny's supervisor asked Jenny to observe Jamilah at Lincoln. Jenny saw clearly that Jamilah was very unhappy and needed intensive services.

Jamilah was given an IQ test to determine whether she should be transferred to Jenny's class at Garland School. The test indicated that Jamilah had low to average intelligence, and there was a great disparity between her verbal score and her performance score. Jamilah's hearing test did not indicate problems. On the basis of her observation and the test results, Jenny recommended that Jamilah transfer.

Mr. and Mrs. Rasheed had been working closely with the kindergarten teacher and recognized that their daughter was severely disabled. However, they had general misgivings about whether IQ tests were valid measurements for inner-city African-American children. Additionally, they had three concerns about Jenny's recommendation. First, at five and a half years old, Jamilah would be the youngest child in Jenny's first–second-grade class—and arguably too young for it.

Second, they were unsure whether it made sense to uproot her from her local school and transport her eight miles to an unfamiliar area of the city. Moreover, she would be the only Muslim child at Garland School, and they were concerned about removing her from the reassuring supports of her own community.

Third, they were very proud of Jamilah's advanced reading ability and wanted her pushed forward in that area of strength. However, Jenny's first priority was to help Jamilah develop language and social skills so that she could interact comfortably with others. Right now, Jamilah didn't know how to use language to meet her needs and cried like a two-year-old to get her way. She would certainly be welcome to join a reading group, but Jenny refused to pressure her to advance.

Despite their reservations, the Rasheeds were ultimately swayed by Jenny's convincing arguments and her calm, reassuring manner. Jamilah started at Garland School in January.

NEW BEGINNINGS

Jamilah's adjustment was not easy. When she didn't want to do something, she'd simply turn her chair around, fold her arms, and refuse to participate. "She's like the Bionic Woman in her interactions with other people," Jenny commented to her friend, the school psychologist. If she wanted her own shoes tied, she'd say stiffly like a robot, "Tie your shoe."

Jenny's priority was to help Jamilah to begin to manage her own behavior. Specifically, she wanted to eliminate Jamilah's frequent crying, teach her to follow directions, and help her to work cooperatively in a group.

Jenny used a behavior management chart to show Jamilah her progress in controlling her crying. Unfortunately, Jamilah was an easy scapegoat—the boys enjoyed making her cry. Jenny often had to intervene to protect Jamilah and to help her to use language, rather than tears, to solve her problems.

During this period of mutual adjustment, Jenny unwittingly stepped on the toes of Jamilah's family. For example, Jenny once brought in some clothes, including warm jackets, that her daughter had outgrown to give to one of the poorer children in the class. Jamilah eyed a dress and was captivated with it. When she asked if she could have it, Jenny didn't want to disappoint the little girl. This happened a second and then a third time. By this point, Jenny was feeling uncomfortable about continuing to send home clothes, but Jamilah pouted unhappily if she was denied the clothing she asked for.

Jenny decided to call the girl's parents. After she explained the situation apologetically to Jamilah's mother, Mrs. Rasheed primly responded that Jamilah's grandmother bought her plenty of clothes. She politely explained that because their religion emphasized self-sufficiency, she did not want her daughter to be given handouts. It had not occurred to Jenny that she might be offending anyone by complying with a little girl's seemingly innocent request. "When I look back on that, it was so insulting to the family," said Jenny.

Another time, Jenny shared a story from a children's magazine with Jamilah. Since the main character's name was Jamilah, she thought it would appeal to the young child. A few days later, Jamilah returned the story with a copy of a letter her parents had sent to the editor. They felt that the author had attributed the customs of Muslims in the Middle East, where women traditionally have subordinate roles, to American Muslims, where independence is stressed. Jenny reread the story and now understood the family's concern; she knew she would have to be more sensitive to their cultural and religious customs.

THE PLANNING AND PLACEMENT TEAM MEETING

In May, Jamilah turned six and her placement for next year had to be decided. Jenny thought that Jamilah should spend half of her day in Jenny's class and half of her day in a regular kindergarten. She was pleased that Jamilah was ready for mainstreaming and felt that the regular kindergarten would provide an opportunity for plenty of informal talking and interaction with other children.

Mr. Rasheed was working, but Mrs. Rasheed attended the PPT meeting. Jenny, the resource teacher, the speech-language pathologist, and the principal were also there. Mrs. Rasheed explained that both she and her husband wanted their daughter to go on to first grade. After all, she was certainly reading at the first-grade level and they didn't want her to fall behind. They thought she should be pushed harder in mathematics, too. Furthermore, they wanted her to return to Lincoln, her neighborhood school.

Jenny felt she had to take a stand. In her opinion, Jamilah would benefit most from a play-oriented setting. She was having difficulty in math and needed many more experiences playing informally with objects—sorting and classifying them—before she could move on to more abstract operations. She didn't even like to count items now. Moreover, she had some motor problems. Her handwriting was unusual, and at recess she couldn't skip or jump easily.

Essentially, Jenny thought that school should not be a struggle for Jamilah. She was still so frustrated by failure. Jenny assumed that if Jamilah were in a class where she could comfortably handle the required tasks, she would grow more self-confident. Once her social skills improved, the academic learning would naturally follow. Jenny reassured Mrs. Rasheed that Jamilah's reading wouldn't backslide.

Mrs. Rasheed listened attentively to Jenny's position and finally agreed. "We trust you," she said.

JAMILAH'S SECOND AND THIRD YEARS AT GARLAND

Although Jamilah was classified as a first grader, she spent the mornings in Jenny's class and the afternoons in the regular kindergarten class during her second year at Garland. The arrangement worked well, and the kindergarten teacher saw Jamilah as a leader. Except for occasional moody periods when she became frustrated or angry, Jamilah loved conversing, socializing, and working cooperatively with others.

For her third year, Jamilah was placed in the second grade. She still spent most of her time in Jenny's first–second-grade special education class but was mainstreamed for at least 10 hours a week in a regular second grade. She had bypassed first grade since she was old enough to be a second grader, was reading at the second-grade level, and her social skills had improved considerably. She adjusted well to second grade.

DECEMBER'S PARENT-TEACHER CONFERENCE, JAMILAH'S THIRD YEAR

Mr. and Mrs. Rasheed expressed their gratitude and appreciation to the teachers and staff who had been so caring and effective in working with their daughter. For next year, they wanted her to return to Lincoln School. Mrs. Rasheed had been volunteering a few hours a week at Lincoln. They knew and liked the school and wanted their daughter back in her own community.

Jenny was taken aback. She had planned that Jamilah would move next year from her class to Mrs. Fineman's second–third-grade special education language class. To recognize her potential, Jamilah needed at least two more years of intensive language instruction in addition to her mainstreamed classroom experience.

The speech-language pathologist and other specialists working with Jamilah also had grave misgivings about the Rasheed's intentions and felt Jamilah needed to stay at Garland. They pointed out that her affect was still unusual. For example, she used stock phrases at times, irrespective of the circumstances. If a child said, "My dog died yesterday," Jamilah might respond, "Oh, that's great!" Her voice inflection was not always appropriate. She raised her pitch at the end of most sentences, even when she wasn't asking a question.

Jenny was torn. A family has the right to choose a school for their child and, knowing the Rasheeds well by this time, Jenny understood their strong desire to have their daughter go to school with other Muslim children. Yet she knew that Lincoln School would not provide the special services that Garland could. Moreover, the children at Lincoln were poorer, scored less well on standardized tests, and might provide a less rich language setting for Jamilah to learn in.

On the other hand, perhaps Jamilah would converse *more* in a setting that was consistent culturally with her family. Jenny was not sure what her recommendation to the Rasheeds should be at the next PPT in June.

Discussion Questions

1. In the largest sense, what dilemma does Jenny face?
2. What are some of the specific underlying issues in this problem?

3. How is the situation viewed from Jenny's perspective? From Mr. and Mrs. Rasheed's perspective?
4. How do you think Jamilah feels?
5. How do you feel about Jamilah's program as it has been so far? Please explain.
   * Should Jamilah have been transferred to a more inclusive setting earlier? If so, at what point? Why?
6. How might cultural or religious differences between teachers and parents create problems in their relationship?
   * How can teachers sensitize themselves to cultural and religious differences among children, parents, and teachers?
   * Should Jenny have incorporated more aspects of the Muslim culture into the curriculum? Why or why not?
7. If you were Jenny, what recommendations would you make at the PPT in June?
   * Would you give first priority to the parents' wishes or the child's needs? Are these mutually exclusive?

Suggested Activities

1. Role-play the PPT meeting in June. Work in trios and alternate the roles of Jenny and Mr. and Mrs. Rasheed. What are the concerns of each? Which are similar and which are different?
2. Interview a teacher who has worked with children with communication disorders. What concerns have parents expressed? How has the teacher responded to these? In what other ways has the teacher worked with the parents?
3. Review multicultural curricula to identify activities or ideas that might have been helpful to Jenny, Jamilah, the Rasheeds, and the other children in the class.

A Lack of Communication

CHARACTERS

Special education teacher:	Cynthia Morehouse
Third-grade teacher:	Margaret Mason
Aide:	Amy Stark
Student:	Emily Janson
Parents:	Diane Janson and
	Larry Mulrone
Mother's boyfriend:	Bob Mitchell

Cynthia, a teacher of the deaf and hearing impaired, put down the phone and sighed. She had received a call from the mother of one of her students, Emily Janson. Emily's grandfather had just died, and Ms. Janson asked Cynthia to break the news to her daughter because she was unable to explain it to her.

Although Cynthia had repeatedly recommended that Ms. Janson take signing classes and had even offered to teach her, Ms. Janson hadn't followed up on her suggestions. The mother communicated to her daughter using a few signs and mostly gestures. It broke Cynthia's heart. "This mother's life was her young child, yet she couldn't communicate with her," she commented.

THE SCHOOL, COMMUNITY, AND TEACHER

Although some children were eligible for free lunches and others lived in the fine homes on the north side of town, the town of Compton was primarily middle class. It was about 10 miles away from a midsized metropolitan area, but it had a rural quality. There were fields, woods, and some poultry farms, as well as two small shopping centers and a small industrial park.

Long Acres School had approximately 600 students in kindergarten through sixth grade. There were two special education teachers, each of whom had a self-contained resource room. Cynthia Morehouse was the teacher of the deaf and hearing impaired.

Cynthia had been teaching for 20 years. After studying speech pathology and audiology as an undergraduate, she volunteered at a rehabilitation center's preschool for children who were deaf. She loved her work and decided to train as a teacher of the deaf. After completing a new federally funded master's program for deaf education at a local university, she went to work. For 17 years, she taught in a program for children with hearing impairments at a regional educational service center designed to provide special services for towns that couldn't afford these services on their own.

Cynthia had come to Compton three years earlier, when the town began its own program for the deaf and hearing impaired. Previously, children had been bused to regional programs. Compton launched the new program largely at the impetus of one parent, who had organized others with children who were deaf and hearing impaired to lobby the board of education to bring the children back to their own community.

Cynthia worked with children whose hearing losses ranged from mild–moderate to severe–profound. All of the children used an auditory training system. The classroom teacher wore a wireless microphone and the students wore a wireless receiver which maintained the volume of the teacher's voice at a comfortable level, no matter what the background noise in the classroom. Some of the children were oral communicators and some used both signing and voice communication. A child's mode of communication was generally determined by the recommendations of an evaluation team and the parents' wishes.

Whenever possible, Cynthia worked with the children in their regular classrooms. She liked working in an inclusive setting and was pleased with the collaborations she had developed with the regular teachers. Depending on the children's needs, she taught some individually outside the classroom for periods from a half hour to two and a half hours. She taught all areas of the curriculum and had a full-time aide, Amy Stark, who interpreted and helped in other ways. In addition to Emily, Cynthia taught four other children.

Cynthia was in the process of completing her sixth-year diploma in administration and supervision. She worked hard, juggling the many demands of her career and her own family of three children and her husband, who was a doctor.

THE CHILD AND FAMILY

Cynthia started working with Emily when she was in third grade. She did not know the cause of Emily's profound hearing loss. The previous year, Emily had been in a self-contained classroom in a nearby town where she was mainstreamed only for special activities such as art.

When Diane Janson became pregnant with Emily, she dropped out of high school. She had never married Emily's father and was angry at him for not being involved in their daughter's life. Although she and Emily lived alone, Diane's father and sister were available to help. Emily was very attached to her grandfather and her aunt. Her aunt stayed with her after school while her mother worked part-time as a sales clerk in a store. Cynthia sensed that Ms. Janson might have low intelligence and that Emily's intelligence might be higher than her mother's.

None of Emily's family could communicate with her except in a minimal manner. They knew only a few signs and used mostly gestures. Emily had hearing aids for both ears but didn't like to wear them, and her mother didn't encourage her to do so. Thus, at school, where she wore a receiver, Emily heard speech. At home, in effect, she didn't, but spent hours in front of the television or playing video games.

Cynthia didn't know why the family hadn't followed her suggestion to come to the signing classes that she held for the teachers and others. Nonetheless, Ms. Janson frequently spoke caringly about Emily, saying, "Emily is all I have," and "This is my child and I love her."

THIRD GRADE

Cynthia met every day with Emily's regular teacher, Margaret Mason, to share suggestions and strategies for helping Emily academically, socially, and emotionally. Emily worked at grade level in math, except on word problems. In the other curricular areas, she was two to three years below grade level. Cynthia pointed out that, nationally, students who were deaf read two to three years behind their peers.

To encourage social relationships, Cynthia taught sign language to all of the third graders in Emily's class. Emily was paired with children for activities. She tried to strike up friendships with some of the children, but they didn't last. She seemed immature socially.

She relied on reading facial expressions to communicate and often assumed that the children were making fun of her when they were actually talking about something else. This led to hurt feelings and even fights. She was becoming a signer who chose not to use her speech—even though both her previous and current programs emphasized a total communication program (both oral communication and signing).

As the year went on, Cynthia became increasingly concerned about Emily. Cynthia thought Emily was getting the best academic program possible in the setting and was meeting the goals of her individualized education plan (IEP) although she was not performing at grade level. However, she was beginning to withdraw. Both Cynthia and Margaret Mason were very concerned that Emily was suffering emotionally. Kids stopped her in the hall to say plaintively, "Mrs. Morehouse, we try to talk to Emily but she won't talk back to us."

At the final parent-teacher conference in the spring near the end of third grade, Cynthia shared her concerns with Emily's mother. She described Emily's social immaturity and need for peers who were deaf. She gently suggested that Diane might want to consider other programs. She alluded to the school for the deaf, a primarily residential program with a small group of day students about ninety minutes away. However, Diane reacted strongly. "I'll never look at that school. Kids from there come into the store and say it's a horrible place and there's a lot of fighting," she retorted. "Emily is all I have."

Cynthia had tried to lay the groundwork for this discussion carefully. Earlier in the year, to make sure Diane understood, she described her observations of Emily in simple terms and then provided a follow-up written explanation. But Diane's communications with Cynthia had always been uneven. She hadn't come to the February conference, nor had she visited the school on Parents' Observation Day. While Cynthia certainly understood Diane's attachment to Emily, she was afraid that the mother was putting her own needs ahead of her daughter's needs.

AN EVENTFUL SUMMER

During the summer between Emily's third- and fourth-grade years, Diane's boyfriend, Bob Mitchell, moved in with her. Now, Cynthia speculated, Diane had someone else to pay attention to. Emily may have felt left out, since neither Diane nor Bob knew enough sign language to communicate effectively with her. Yet Bob was attentive to the young girl, and Emily enjoyed him. He would take her for bike rides, and they built together with Legos.

Then, one day, a terrible accident occurred. Emily and her aunt were driving home from the park, and their car was hit by a drunk driver and rolled over. Although her aunt was unscathed, Emily's injuries were so bad that she had to spend several weeks during the summer in the hospital.

As Cynthia pointed out, this experience alone would have been traumatic for any child. But Emily not only had to contend with the physical trauma and the hospitalization, she didn't know what was going on and could communicate with no one. Luckily, Cynthia was available to tutor her in the hospital and to interpret for her, at least while she was visiting. Still, Emily was terribly frightened.

FOURTH GRADE

After this traumatic summer, Emily faced more turmoil at home during her fourth-grade year. Her father, Larry Mulrone, had recently married, and he and his new wife wanted to be involved in Emily's life. Although he'd had little previous contact, he now demanded to see his daughter and to review her school records. Cynthia could not release the records to him because he did not have legal guardianship. Emily's mother was resentful of the father's belated interest. "He'd always promised to take her out before, but he never did," she commented ruefully to Cynthia. Cynthia was not sure how often Emily actually saw her father now.

Even more upsetting was the death of Emily's grandfather. He had been a constant and comforting presence in her life since birth. They had enjoyed cooking and taking walks together. Emily seemed to be bereft and drifting emotionally.

Cynthia looked for ways to ease her distress. The school psychologist recommended some children's stories dealing with separation, loss, and death. Although Cynthia read these to Emily and tried to use them as a springboard for her to express her feelings, she didn't talk much. Her sign language was limited, and Cynthia felt that her feelings were bottled inside of her.

Unfortunately, Emily had no one to share her grief with except Cynthia and her aide. Her mother, her aunt, and Bob still had not learned to communicate effectively with her. In fact, toward the end of fourth grade, Emily would ask Cynthia to write notes to her mother about important things she wanted to tell Diane. When Cynthia urged her to talk to Diane, she'd shake her head sadly and respond, "She doesn't understand."

The classroom situation had not improved for Emily. At the PPT meeting at the end of third-grade, Cynthia had recommended keeping Emily's entire third grade class together for fourth grade, so her peer group would remain the same. She was delighted when her principal agreed to this unusual request.

Cynthia and Margaret Mason continued to try various ways to help Emily feel part of the group and to enhance her language development. For example, in addition to teaching signing to the class and pairing Emily with other children, they made sure that she had a friend to sit with in the cafeteria. At the class's musical performance, one of the songs was signed. On the playground, Cynthia explained the rules of basketball to Emily so that she could join in the play. However, the other fourth graders' interests had changed, and for the most part they no longer liked the same kinds of play that Emily enjoyed. More and more, Emily seemed to be alone.

To encourage friendships, Cynthia taught advanced signing once a week to the students and Margaret Mason. Yet when Emily's classmates used sign language to talk with her, she turned away. On the playground, while the kids were playing tag or dodge ball, she wandered off alone.

What few interactions there were tended to be fights. Because of communication difficulties, Emily presumed that children were making hurtful comments when they weren't, as far as her teachers could tell. She responded with angry pushing and shoving.

Since the teachers couldn't communicate effectively with Emily either, Cynthia or Amy, her aide, were called to resolve the disputes. Cynthia was more than willing to help and saw this as part of her responsibilities. However, she began to feel more strongly that Long Acres School was not the right place for Emily and that she wasn't getting an appropriate education. There was more to life than just academics.

Parent conferences were held three times a year. By the end of fourth grade, Cynthia again hoped to get Diane to consider the school for the deaf for Emily. In her communications during the course of the year, she began to plant the seeds for this.

In fourth grade, Emily was due for a psychoeducational evaluation, required by law every three years for children receiving special education. This generally included an assessment of academic achievement, social behavior, intelligence, perceptual-motor skills, self-image, vision, hearing, and other appropriate areas. Cynthia requested the evaluation in September because she knew that it often took several months for them to be arranged. She also requested that the evaluator be from the school for the deaf, because she felt no one in her system was qualified to evaluate a deaf child who signed. Emily's last evaluation, three years earlier, had been done at the school for the deaf, and they would have her previous evaluation as a basis for comparison. Along with this request, Cynthia sent a detailed report of Emily's academic performance and her concerns about her social and emotional development.

PREPARING FOR THE SPRING PLANNING AND PLACEMENT MEETING

In May, a PPT meeting would be held to determine Emily's placement for her fifth-grade year. Cynthia suspected that Emily's psychoevaluation would support her conviction that she should attend the school for the deaf. But the bureaucratic process often grinds slowly—and the evaluation still hadn't taken place. The PPT was scheduled in two weeks.

Cynthia felt she needed extra support to convince Diane that the school for the deaf was the right move for Emily. Whenever she had gently raised the possibility, Diane had rejected it. Although her opposition became less strident, Diane still saw it as "sending her daughter away" and couldn't envision it, either for Emily or herself.

Cynthia was caught in a dilemma. She had to make a recommendation at the PPT for Emily's placement next year. Should she take a firm stand and forcefully propose the school for the deaf? Perhaps Diane would be convinced in a formal meeting if other professionals were present to support the idea.

However, Diane was skittish. A direct statement from Cynthia in front of others might make Diane dig in her heels. And Cynthia was just beginning to make headway—Diane seemed to be softening her position. Perhaps by the end of fifth grade, Diane would be more ready to accept the idea. On the other hand, could Emily afford to wait that long?

Discussion Questions

1. What is Cynthia's overall dilemma?
   - What are the underlying issues?

2. How might the situation be viewed by Diane Janson? By Emily? By Margaret Mason?

3. What might be keeping Emily's mother from learning how to communicate effectively with her?

4. Evaluate Cynthia's efforts at communicating with Emily's mother? What other strategies might she have tried?
   - Should Ms. Mason have been more involved?
   - What about other professionals, such as the school psychologist?

5. Do you think Emily would have been more able to benefit from an inclusive setting if she had not encountered so many difficulties at home? Please explain.
   - Are there other recommendations that might help Emily's home situation?
   - What other resources might be available to help at home? Should Cynthia suggest these to Diane?

6. What should Cynthia recommend at the PPT?
   - How pressing is the problem? Should she strongly propose the school for the deaf this year, or would it be better to wait for next year?

Suggested Activities

1. Role-play the May PPT meeting, at which Cynthia makes the recommendation for next year for Emily. Role-play the roles of the principal, the speech-language pathologist, the school psychologist, Cynthia, and Margaret Mason.

2. Write a research paper on the different approaches to teaching children who are deaf and hearing impaired to communicate. Investigate the controversy between advocates of American Sign Language and advocates of a total communication program.

3. Visit a residential or day school for deaf children. What are the goals of the school? What is the curriculum like? How does the school work with hearing parents of children who are deaf?

Selected Readings

COMMUNICATING WITH FAMILIES

Abbot, C. F., and S. Gold. 1991. Conferring with parents when you're concerned that their child needs special services. *Young Children* 46(4): 10–20.

Berger, E. H. 1995. Communication and parent programs. In *Parents as partners in education: Families and schools working together*, pp. 159–203. Englewood Cliffs, NJ: Prentice-Hall.

Brooks, J. B. 1994. *Parenting in the 90s.* Mountain View, CA: Mayfield Publishing Company.

Epstein, J. L. 1986. Parents' reactions to teacher practices of parent involvement. *Elementary School Journal* 86(3): 277–294.

Galinsky, E. 1990. Why are some parent/teacher partnerships clouded with difficulties? *Young Children* 45(5): 2–3, 38–39.

Gestwicki, C. 1992. Techniques for developing partnerships. In *Home, school and community relations*, pp. 153–281. Albany, NY: Delmar Publishers.

Heath, H. E. 1994. Dealing with difficult behaviors: Teachers plan with parents. *Young Children* 49(5): 20–24.

McLoughlin, C. S. 1987. *Parent-teacher conferencing.* Springfield, IL: Thomas.

Morgan, E. L. 1989. Talking with parents when concerns come up. *Young Children* 44(2): 52–56.

Powell, D. R. 1990. Research in review: Home visiting in the early years: Policy and program decisions. *Young Children* 45(6): 65–73.

Rotter, J. C., and E. H. Robinson. 1986. *Parent-teacher conferencing: What research says to the teacher.* Washington, DC: National Education Association.

Spewock, T. S. 1991. Teaching parents of young children through learning packets. *Young Children* 47(1): 28–31.

Stone, J. G. 1987. *Teacher-parent relationships.* Washington, DC: NAEYC.

Swap, S. M. 1987. Making conferences productive. In *Enhancing parent involvement in schools*, pp. 35–51. New York: Teachers College Press.

FAMILY PARTICIPATION IN SCHOOLS

Berger, E. H. 1995. *Parents as partners in education: Families and schools working together.* Englewood Cliffs, NJ: Prentice-Hall.

Boutte, G. S., D. L. Keepler, U. S. Tyler, and B. Z. Terry. 1992. Effective techniques for involving "difficult" parents. *Young Children* 47(3): 19–22.

Cataldo, C. Z. 1987. *Parent education for early childhood: Child-rearing concepts and program content for the student and practicing professional.* New York: Teachers College Press.

Cochran, M., and C. Dean. 1991. Home-school relations and the empowerment process. *Elementary School Journal* 91(3): 261–69.

Comer, J. P., and N. M. Haynes. 1991. Parent involvement in schools: An ecological approach. *Elementary School Journal* 91(3): 271–77.

Davies, D., P. Burch, and V. R. Johnson. 1992. *A portrait of schools reaching out: Report of a survey of practices and policies of family-community-school collaboration.* Boston: Institute for Responsive Education (ERIC Document Reproduction Service No. 343 701).

Epstein, J. L. 1995. School/family/community partnerships: Caring for the children we share. *Phi Delta Kappan* 76(9): 701–12.

Frahm, R. A. 1994. The failure of Connecticut's reform plan: Lessons for the nation. *Phi Delta Kappan* 76(2): 156–59.

Galen, H. 1991. Increasing parent involvement in elementary school: The nitty-gritty of one successful program. *Young Children* 46(2): 18–22.

Henderson, A. T., and N. Berla, eds. 1994. *A new generation of evidence: The family is critical to student achievement.* Washington, DC: National Committee for Citizens in Education (ERIC Document Reproduction Service No. 375 968).

Kagan, S. L., and P. Neville. 1993. *Integrating services for children and families: Understanding the past to shape the future.* New Haven, CT: Yale University Press.

Kochan, F. K., and C. D. Herrington. 1992. Restructuring for today's children: Strengthening schools by strengthening families. *Educational Forum* 57(1): 42–49.

McConnell, B. B. 1991. *Evaluation of the Parent Leadership Training Program.* Seattle, WA: Citizens Education Center (ERIC Document Reproduction Service No. 338 415).

Powell, D. R. 1989. *Families and early childhood programs.* Washington, DC: NAEYC.

Rich, D. 1987. *Schools and families: Issues and actions.* Washington, DC: National Education Association.

Stone, C. R. 1995. School/community collaboration. *Phi Delta Kappan* 76(10): 794–800.

Swap, S. M. 1987. *Enhancing parent involvement in schools.* New York: Teachers College Press.

Swick, K. J. 1991. *Teacher-Parent partnerships to enhance school success in early childhood education.* Washington, DC: National Education Association.

United States Department of Education 1994. *Strong families, strong schools: Building community partnerships for learning.* Washington, DC: U.S. Department of Education.

WORKING WITH FAMILIES OF AT-RISK CHILDREN AND CHILDREN WITH SPECIAL NEEDS

Bailey, D. B. 1994. Working with families of children with special needs. In M. Wolery and J. S. Wilbers, eds., *Including children with special needs in early childhood programs*, pp. 23–44. Washington, DC: NAEYC.

Barr, R. D. and W. H. Parrett. 1995. Programs that work: Early childhood and elementary schools. In *Hope at last for at-risk youth*, pp. 64–94. Boston, MA: Allyn and Bacon.

Bjorck-Akesson, E., and M. Granlund. 1995. Family involvement in assessment and intervention: Perceptions of professionals and parents in Sweden. *Exceptional Children* 61(6): 520–535.

Bronheim, S. 1990. *An Educator's Guide to Tourette Syndrome.* Bayside, NY: Tourette Syndrome Association (ERIC Document Reproduction Service No. ED 321 467).

Brooks, J. B. 1994. Parenting at times of change and trauma. In *Parenting in the 90's*, pp. 254–93. Mountain View, CA: Mayfield Publishing Company.

Cook, R. E., A. Tessier, and M. D. Klein. 1992. *Adapting early childhood curricula for children with special needs.* NY: Merrill.

Council for Exceptional Children 1994. *Inclusion: Ensuring appropriate services to children and youth with emotional/behavioral disorders.* Reston, VA: Council for Exceptional Children.

——— 1992. *Children with ADD: A shared responsibility: Based on a report of the Council for Exceptional Children's Task Force on Children with Attention Deficit Disorder.* Reston, VA: Council for Exceptional Children.

Ebenstein, B. 1995. IEP strategies. *Exceptional Parent*, 25(4): 62–63.

Garbarino, J. 1987. Family support and the prevention of child maltreatment. In S. L. Kagan, D. R. Powell, B. Weissbourd, and E. F. Zigler, eds., *America's family support programs*, pp. 99–114. New Haven, CT: Yale University Press.

Green, S. K., and M. R. Shinn. 1994. Parent attitudes about special education and reintegration: What is the role of student outcomes? *Exceptional Children* 61(3): 269–81.

Hollowood, T. M., C. L. Salisbury, B. Rainforth, and M. M. Palombaro. 1994. Use of instructional time in classrooms serving students with and without severe disabilities. *Exceptional Children* 62(3): 242–53.

Manning, M. L., and L. G. Baruth. 1995. Parents and families of at-risk students. In *Students at risk*, pp. 237–59. Boston: Allyn and Bacon.

Miller, L. J., P. S. Strain, K. Boyd, S. Hunsicker, J. McKinley, and A. Wu. 1992. Parental attitudes towards integration. *Topics in Early Childhood Special Education* 12: 230–46.

National information and advocacy resources. 1995. *Exceptional Parent* 25(1): 5–8.

Olweus, D. 1993. *Bullying at school: What we know and what we can do.* Cambridge, MA: Blackwell Publishers.

Osborne, A. G., Jr., and P. Dimattia. 1994. The IDEA's least restrictive environment mandate: Legal implications. *Exceptional Children* 61(1): 6–14.

Shames, G. H., and E. H. Wiig. 1990. *Human communication disorders.* New York: Macmillan.

Siegel, L. M. 1994. *Least restrictive environment: The paradox of inclusion.* Horsham, PA: LRP Publications.

Swick, K. J., and S. P. Graves. 1993. *Empowering at-risk families during the early childhood years.* Washington, DC: National Education Association.

White, K. R., M. J. Taylor, and V. D. Moss. 1992. Does research support claims about the benefits of involving parents in early intervention programs? *Review of Educational Research* 62(1): 91–125.

Wiegerink, R., and M. Comfort. 1987. Parent involvement: Support for families of children with special needs. In S. L. Kagan, D. R. Powell, B. Weissbourd, and E. F. Zigler, eds., *America's Family Support Programs,* pp. 182–206. New Haven, CT: Yale University Press.

Yell, M. L. 1995. The least restrictive environment mandate and the courts: Judicial activism or judicial restraint? *Exceptional Children* 61(6): 578–81.

WORKING WITH CULTURALLY DIVERSE FAMILIES

Abt Associates. 1991. *Working with families: Promising programs to help parents support young children's learning: Summary findings.* Washington, DC: U.S. Government Printing Office.

Comer, J. P. 1988. Educating poor minority children. *Scientific American* 259: 42–46.

Davidson, B. M. 1993. *School restructuring: A study of the role of parents in selected accelerated schools.* Paper presented at the Annual Meeting of the Mid-South Educational Research Association, New Orleans, LA.

Epstein, J. L. and S. L. Dauber. 1991. School programs and teacher practices of parent involvement in inner city elementary and middle schools. *Elementary School Journal* 91(3): 289–305.

Fine, M. 1993. [Ap]parent involvement: Reflections on parents, power, and urban public schools. *Teachers College Record* 94(4): 682–710.

Harry, B., N. Allen, and M. McLaughlin. 1995. Communication versus compliance: African-American parents' involvement in special education. *Exceptional Children* 61(4): 364–77.

Igoa, C. 1995. *The inner world of the immigrant child*. New York: St. Martin's Press.

Lee, F. Y. 1995. Asian parents as partners. *Young Children* 50(3): 4–8.

Nettles, S. M. 1991. Community involvement and disadvantaged students: A review. *Review of Educational Research* 61(3): 379–406.

Neugebauer, B., ed. 1987. *Alike and different: Exploring our humanity with young children*. Redmond, WA: Exchange Press.

Smylie, M. A., R. L. Crowson, V. Chou, and R. A. Levin. 1994. The principal and community-school connections in Chicago's radical reform. *Educational Administration Quarterly* 30(3): 342–64.

Williams, K. 1987. Cultural diversity in family support. In S. L. Kagan. D. R. Powell, B. Weissbourd, and E. F. Zigler, eds., *America's family support programs*, pp. 295–307. New Haven, CT: Yale University Press.

COLLABORATION AMONG PROFESSIONALS

Baker, E. T., M. C. Wang, and H. J. Walberg. 1995. Synthesis of research: The effects of inclusion on learning. *Educational Leadership* 52(4): 33–35.

Bruder, M. B. 1994. Working with members of other disciplines: Collaboration for success. In M. Wolery and J. S. Wilbers, eds., *Including children with special needs in early childhood programs*, pp. 45–70. Washington, DC: NAEYC.

Elliot, S. N. and S. M. Sheridan. 1992. Consultation and teaming: Problem solving among educators, parents, and support personnel. *Elementary School Journal* 92(3): 315–338.

Fuchs, D., and L. S. Fuchs. 1994. Inclusive schools movement and the radicalization of special education reform. *Exceptional Children* 60(4): 294–309.

Gage, J., and S. Workman. 1994. Creating family support systems: In Head Start and beyond. *Young Children* 49(7): 74–77.

Janney, R. E., M. E. Snell, M. K. Beers, and M. Raynes. 1995. Integrating students with moderate and severe disabilities into general education classes. *Exceptional Children* 61(5): 425–39.

Jones, M. M., and L. L. Carlier. 1995. Creating inclusionary opportunities for learners with multiple disabilities. *Teaching Exceptional Children* 27(3): 23–27.

Kagan, S. L. 1991. *United we stand: Collaboration in child care and early education services*. New York: Teachers College Press.

Kagan, S. L., and A. M. Rivera. 1991. Collaboration in early care and education: What can and should we expect? *Young Children* 47(1): 51–56.

Phillips, V., and L. McCullough. 1990. Consultation-based programming: Instituting the collaborative ethic in schools. *Exceptional Children* 56(4): 291–301.

Powell, D. R. 1991. How schools support families: Critical policy tensions. *Elementary School Journal* 91(3): 307–19.

Putnam, J. W., A. N. Spiegel, and R. H. Bruininks. 1995. Future directions in education and inclusion of students with disabilities: A Delphi investigation. *Exceptional Children* 61(6): 553–76.

Wang, M. C., M. C. Reynolds, and H. J. Walberg. 1995. Serving students at the margins. *Educational Leadership* 52(4): 12–17.

Wolery, M. 1994. Assessing children with special needs. In M. Wolery and J. S. Wilbers, eds., *Including children with special needs in early childhood programs*, pp. 71–96. Washington, DC: NAEYC.